PLAYING THE CHANGES

PLAYING THE CHANGES

A Musician's Memoir

COLIN JAMES

RANDOM HOUSE CANADA

PUBLISHED BY RANDOM HOUSE CANADA

 Published in 2026 by Random House Canada, a division of Penguin Random House Canada Limited, Toronto.

Random House Canada, an imprint of Penguin Random House Canada Limited
320 Front Street West, Suite 1400
Toronto, Ontario, M5V 3B6, Canada
penguinrandomhouse.ca

The authorized representative in the EU for product safety and compliance is Penguin Random House Ireland, Morrison Chambers, 32 Nassau Street, Dublin D02 YH68, Ireland. https://eu-contact.penguin.ie

Library and Archives Canada Cataloguing in Publication

Title: Playing the changes: a musician's memoir / Colin James.
Names: James, Colin (Guitarist), author
Identifiers: Canadiana (print) 20260120286 | Canadiana (ebook) 20260121061 | ISBN 9781039013261 (hardcover) | ISBN 9781039013278 (EPUB)
Subjects: LCSH: James, Colin (Guitarist)—Childhood and youth. | LCSH: Singers—Canada—Biography. | LCSH: Guitarists—Canada—Biography. | LCSH: Blues musicians—Canada—Biography. | LCSH: Rock musicians—Canada—Biography. | LCGFT: Autobiographies.
Classification: LCC ML420.J29 A3 2026 | DDC 782.42164092—dc23

Text design: Matthew Flute
Cover design: Matthew Flute
Image credits: Courtesy of the author
Typesetting: Arthur Dennyson Hamdani and Six Red Marbles
Interior photos: Courtesy of the author

Printed in Canada

2 4 6 8 9 7 5 3 1

Penguin
Random House
RANDOM HOUSE CANADA

For Mom and Dad

CONTENTS

PROLOGUE

WHAT DO YOU COOK when Joni Mitchell comes for dinner? This was the question my wife Heather and I faced one Saturday night in 1991. I'd known Joni forever, of course, but only through her music. *Blue* came out when I was six years old, and it had been one of the soundtracks of my childhood, growing up in a little house in Regina where music was always playing. My parents loved Joni's records, so I did too. I'd been lucky enough to have a drink with her the night before in Vancouver, when I met up with her and her boyfriend, the musician Don Freed, at a little spot in Kitsilano. Don is himself a gifted singer-songwriter and I'd known him for a long time. I'd even been his sideman years back, once driving all the way to Montreal when I was eighteen to play a gig that was, let's say, somewhat under-attended. On that same trip we'd stop in Toronto so Don could record with Jane Siberry's band, and I'd meet Jeff Healey for the first time, who'd befriended my sister, Cathy, while she studied at the Ontario College of Art.

We'd met up with Joni and Don in a bar where everybody recognized her, but they were all cool enough not to show it. Joni is incredible; she's unlike anybody else you've ever met. She just says things, totally unexpected things, and you can't help but roll with it. She's Joni! What else are you going to do? She'll look at an outlet in the wall and say she can see the electricity coming out of it. And you just nod along like, *yes, absolutely, of course you can.*

But a beer in a Kitsilano bar is a very different thing from a dinner in Lions Bay, one being held in the little wooden house Heather and I had bought the year before. It was, and still is, I think, the smallest one in town. Inside the house was all cedar; it smelled amazing and made you feel as if you were in a cozy little tree house. Lions Bay sits north of Vancouver, on the eastern shore of Howe Sound, and pretty much everywhere you could build a home there has a stunning vista in front of it. Joni was coming for dinner along with Don, my manager, Steve Macklam, and his wife, Caroline. Steve had a very small roster of talent at that time, consisting of myself and the Chieftains, and would, perhaps not coincidentally, sign up Joni herself not long after that evening at our place. So we had a nice guest list and a beautiful view, but we kept coming back to our big problem: What do you cook for a living legend?

Heather settled on a curry chicken dish with grapes, a recipe borrowed from a hotel in LA. I remember thinking at the time that chicken and grapes seemed kind of a crazy combo to me, but it must have been the right call, because Joni had seconds that night. We all sat around, talking about music and life, and taking in the view of Howe Sound, Vancouver Island visible in the distance along with Hutt, Bowen, and Gambier Islands, then stretching on towards Nanaimo—or at least those of us who could see it, because for some reason Joni sat with her back to the windows, as I recall.

At one point, somebody noticed a guitar leaning against the wall in the corner of the dining room, the only one I had in the house at the time as all my gear was out on the road somewhere. It was a kind of junky old Isana archtop, a model made famous by Elvis, and the very instrument that would a few years later grace the cover of my first record with the Little Big Band. Its presence wasn't intentional, and if I'd thought there was a chance anyone would touch it, I'd have stashed it in a closet. But here was Joni Mitchell, used to playing whatever beautiful vintage Martin she wanted, and all I had to offer her was this funky Isana. I cringed as she took it in her hands, but of course I shouldn't have. She's Joni! She tuned it to one of her beautiful open tunings and started strumming.

If she'd been taking requests, mine would have been "Cotton Avenue," the first track off *Don Juan's Reckless Daughter*. I loved that record. I was thirteen when it came out, and it was the first album of Joni's that I felt I'd discovered myself, instead of having it introduced to me by my parents. But that night Joni had something else in mind, and launched into a song none of us had ever heard—a beautiful, beguiling song wherein each verse ended with the unforgettable line "happiness is the best facelift." Years later she'd release it on her record *Taming the Tiger* as "Face Lift." Here she was, this hero of my youth *and* my adulthood, previewing unreleased work in our dining room, making my bad guitar sound a lot better than it should. And it wasn't just that she was a hero of mine. She was a *Saskatchewan* hero of mine, unquestionably the greatest and most important musician to emerge from the province we'd both grown up in. Joni was from Saskatoon! The very town whose bars I'd played my way through on my way up. And Joni had conquered the world.

Here was Joni Mitchell, proof that the wildest dreams cooked up by a prairie kid could come true. I'd seen her play in her hometown when I was eight years old, with my mom, dad, and siblings, at Centennial Auditorium, the same venue where I'd not too long later open for another hero of mine, Stevie Ray Vaughan, for the first time. On our drive home after the show, Dad lost control of the car and spun off the road into a snowy field. Someone who saw the accident said they saw our tail lights spin around three times as we spiralled to an eventual stop in a snowbank, where we waited in shock until some help arrived from fellow drivers.

And here Joni was at my dining room table. At some point that night she looked at me, one of those looks where you have the feeling the person can see right through you like an X-ray. Like they can read your thoughts, or see your very soul.

"So, Colin," she said. "You're a lifer."

It was halfway between a statement and question. Like she didn't want to presume, but she could tell from being around me. Joni could tell because she knew within herself what it meant to be one, what it felt like. She knew as well as I did that I was in for the long haul, that music was my life, and that I would give my life to it in return. A comment, a question, I'm not sure. But a recognition, an acknowledgement—it was definitely that. She saw flickering in me the same flame that roared in her, and she wanted me to know she saw it.

"You know, Joni, I think I might be. A lifer. Yeah, that's me."

This book is the story of the long road that took me from Regina, Saskatchewan, to being serenaded by Joni Mitchell in our little tree house, and far, far beyond. It's a story of ups and downs, of triumphs and heartbreaks. It's a story of family and friends and a whole lot of music. A story of giving something your all, and learning to be honest with yourself about what you can do and what you want. It's the story of my life. A life in music—a life spent playing the changes.

CHAPTER ONE

MIDDLE OF CANADA

I WAS BORN AT three in the morning on August 17, 1964, as though even then I knew I was in for a lot of late nights. And I was born at home, which perhaps explains why I've always had such a close connection to warm and comfortable domestic spaces, a grounding balance to the wildness of a musician's life on the road. The timing was my own, but I can't claim credit for the home birth. That was down to my mother, Joyce, who wanted it that way. A few years earlier, my older sister had been born during a very busy time at the local hospital, and Mom had had a bad experience. It had been impersonal, her baby being wheeled away as soon as the rushed birth was over. This was in 1960, around the time of a lot of tensions in the hospital system over Saskatchewan's plan to introduce new universal health care. It was a strained moment in the province's history that would eventually lead to a doctors' strike, and Mom never forgot the feeling of lying in the hospital bed alone after labour, having to ask a distracted nurse if her newborn was a boy or a girl. When it was my turn, Mom and her midwife made a different plan, and I was born in a more welcoming setting.

Home then was a small house on McTavish Street in the Cathedral area of Regina, Saskatchewan—so called because of the beautiful Holy Rosary Cathedral that anchored the neighbourhood, built in 1913. The two-spired cathedral is pretty much in the middle of Regina, and Regina is pretty much in the middle of Canada. We lived around the corner from a stately old brick library and a classic barber shop, complete with the candy cane–painted pole outside. In the mid-sixties Regina was a postcard-perfect prairie town, something out of an old TV show—tree-lined streets and tidy houses everywhere. Later I would come to chafe against its smallness and yearn for bigger things, but it was as good a place as any to grow up.

I was the last of four children born to my parents, Joyce and Bill Munn. My siblings, Robbie, Murray, and Cathy, all came before, and were, I believe, all delivered by the same doctor, an Englishman. My mom had discovered she was pregnant with me quite late. She'd gone to the movies with a friend and got so nauseated that she went straight to see the same Dr. Dexter, who told her he was surprised that after having three kids she didn't recognize that she was five months pregnant. She was thirty years old. In the morning, after my middle-of-the-night arrival, my mom woke my older siblings up and brought them in to meet their new baby brother. Robbie, the oldest at seven, looked down at me, then back at my mom, then back down at me. "Mom," he asked, "can we keep him?"

My mom said yes, and so there we were. Two social worker parents, a whack of kids, and the sixties not even halfway over. It was a heady time, with all kinds of ideas and music in the air. We were Quakers, and I was born into a beatnik world of social activism and hippie potlucks. At the time, of course, I knew none of that. I was just the new kid in the house, born into a very particular time. I did probably hear music that first day, though. Something was always on the turntable, and I like to think I was welcomed into this world by one of the artists who filled our home. Maybe it was Pete Seeger. Maybe it was Peter, Paul and Mary. Or maybe it was *Another Side of Bob Dylan*, which was released just nine days before I was born. That's nice to think about, in a way—my first day on earth soundtracked by "Chimes of Freedom" or "It Ain't Me, Babe." I can't say for sure, but I know that when I was born, music was in the air, and so was hopeful change.

Mom and Dad met in the early fifties at what was then called the Weyburn Mental Hospital, where they both worked as nurses. The hospital was, at the time, the home of some very unusual stuff. Lobotomies and electroshock therapy, yes, but also experiments with LSD. In fact, it's where the controversial Dr. Humphry Osmond was running trials using acid to treat schizophrenia, alcoholism, and other conditions.

Osmond actually coined the word *psychedelics*, and my dad was on the front line of this research, having volunteered to try LSD under medical supervision as part of the early trials. What the participants experienced would be mostly just whispered about in family lore, but I do remember my brother Robbie claiming to have read a journal in which Dad recounted seeing flying tigers. Dr. Osmond would later introduce Aldous Huxley to mescaline, and his work at Weyburn would inspire the CIA's famous explorations of LSD in the MKUltra program, a research initiative that would, crazy as it sounds, count the Unabomber, Theodore Kaczynski, as one of its test subjects. By the time I came along, my parents had left the hospital and, as far as I know, had left LSD behind too. Years down the road, I'd get the chance to meet Dr. Osmond in Alabama, but I'll get to that later.

Apart from a sepia-toned memory of getting bitten on the nose by the family dog after taunting him with knitting needles under the couch, I don't recall that house in the Cathedral district very well. We were there for only a few years before moving, eventually settling in a house on 24th Street, which is where I would do most of my growing up. It was a full-on folkie/hippie house, two floors full of homespun pottery and macramé god's-eye wall hangings, butterfly chairs and wax-splattered Mateus wine bottles holding candles, bookshelves built with cinder blocks and boards of pine. In winter, if the snow got deep enough, we would ski out the front door to Wascana Lake or jump off the back of the garage into snowbanks six feet high. The house faced south, and along its west side, between it and the busy Argyle Avenue, was a long, narrow yard. As a kid, it felt like a football field to me, it was so huge. My siblings and I would play catch or Frisbee. Only later, when I visited that house long after moving away, did I realize how small it actually was. It's quite touching how our perception changes as we grow, and as the world around us expands. But in the late sixties, the house on 24th Street was our kingdom, and big enough to hold all our hopes and dreams.

And the four of us kids were full of them, even if they were quite different. Robbie, seven years older, was the big kid. If I were to employ an often-used trope, Robbie would be the long-haired, hard-rocking party guy, sometimes a bit of a hellraiser, but just as likely to get emotionally lost in a Grateful Dead ballad or a song by the California band Hot Tuna. Handsome and charismatic, he was the king of us siblings and an elder in the broader group of cousins, always happy to throw yours truly into a snowbank as he walked away. But in a way, I knew he'd have my back if I needed him.

After Robbie there was Murray, six years older than me, who was different—red-headed while the rest of us had dark hair, a brainiac and probably way better at school than all of us. He was quiet and reserved, but with a real sense of humour, likely to walk into the woods alone, happy to just disappear, but happy, too, to know that we'd all come to look for him.

And last but not least, Cathy, my nearest sibling, just four years older than me. Cathy and I were buddies always, a closeness made easy by our proximity in age, yes, but one cemented by our shared, joyful love of music. Our whole family loved music, I should be clear, but Cathy and I had something special, goofing off and singing together, harmonizing even as kids. I vividly remember being four years old and sitting in her room listening to "Israelites" by Desmond Dekker and the Aces on her tiny little plastic turntable. My brothers by that time were into the Monkees, and I'd later enjoy the use of a hand-me-down lunchbox bearing the smiling faces of Micky, Davy, Michael, and Peter.

My parents were a loving, stable presence in our lives. My mother, Joyce, was born in Weyburn, Saskatchewan, but grew up in the interior of BC. She was an extraordinary person, and had a long and beautiful life. Back when we were growing up, she was an outgoing, vibrant, and stylish woman, and she loomed large in our house. She was worldly and curious, and would eagerly share her new culinary discoveries that she found in *Gourmet* magazine—like pizza, which was still a rarity in Saskatchewan when I was a kid. Mom learned how to make it herself and was known to throw a pizza party, inviting friends and neighbours over to share this exotic treat. She subscribed to *The New Yorker*, and would entertain us all by sharing the cartoons from the magazine.

Mom was a fair-minded and loving parent, and never much of a disciplinarian. I remember once she was trying to berate me for some dumb thing I was doing, but I had started to get a bit bigger, and a bit faster, and so I told her that she wasn't going to be able to stop me—she couldn't catch me even if she tried. Mom got a wooden spoon and chased me through the yard all the way around the house. At some point I slipped back inside and locked myself in the upstairs bathroom. She was mad, but she also saw the futility and humour in it, so her banging on the door with the wooden utensil took on a manic, comic quality. When I finally emerged, shards of wooden spoon were lying everywhere outside the door, like it had been put through a wood chipper. We ended up collapsing on the ground in a heap and laughing our heads off, and she finally agreed that I was too big and too fast to keep in line now.

Mom was passionate about her career as a social worker, and tight with her colleagues, who became her friends and thus had their own roles in our lives. One of them, her boss at family services, Al Mayotte, was into birding, and he took our whole family out to see the whooping cranes, the huge, rare birds that would appear from time to time in Saskatchewan on their way north from wintering in Texas. Al would tell us that the cranes were coming our way for the next week or two, and we'd all go out to observe them in the wild. My mom always loved birds, and so those trips were special. I'd see all of Mom's work friends at her office when I visited, in an old low-rise building downtown, near the post office. And sometimes they'd come over to the house for drinks, and I couldn't help but ham it up. I'd quietly approach the arched entrance to the living room and then do a silly walk all the way across it. They'd all laugh, then I'd disappear and do it again. I guess I always loved an audience. Once, when I was maybe seven or eight, I announced that I wanted to meet my mother downtown for lunch. To her credit, she didn't balk at this preposterous idea, but instead let me bike there alone and happily met me at Woolworth's, not far from her office, where we sat at the lunch counter and had hamburgers. I was so proud to do it—it felt so *adult*—but I was also just so happy to be with her, sharing some fries and a laugh.

My dad, Bill, was a different kind of person—a gangly guy, kind of skinny, and he loved jokes, especially puns. His father had been famous for them, much to the frustration of my grandmother, Jean, who would roll her eyes whenever my grandfather got going in his exaggerated Scottish brogue. The joking tradition continued in our house, on both sides—my father's punning enthusiasm matched by my mother's enthusiastic annoyance with them. Dad was born in Virden, Manitoba, where his father was the local Manitoba union grain man. He had five siblings, and they all ended up in Saskatoon, where dad went to high school at Nutana Collegiate. He also loved jazz music, especially the swinging big band styles that had been popular in his youth. He would often tell stories about seeing Duke Ellington play in Saskatoon in the early fifties, and ultimately befriending one of his musicians, the legendary Billy Strayhorn, after the show. At that time only Duke himself was allowed to stay at Saskatoon's premier hotel, the Bessborough; unfortunately, back then most African Americans could not assume they'd be able to stay at a given hotel. My dad innocently offered his new friend and others a place to party. Sadly, when they both arrived at my grandparents' house on Lorne Street, they refused to let Billy stay the night.

I never had the sense that my father was happy in his work. He settled into a government job as a personnel director after doing social work. I thought it must have been incredibly boring, because there was never any talk of it at home, unlike Mom's work, which we heard a lot about. But Dad came alive through his hobbies. He was a gifted photographer, and loved to take pictures of all sorts of things—prairie landscapes, train cars, and folk musicians (which I'm sure played its part in delivering me to some formative early musical experiences, as I accompanied my parents to folk concerts around town). He'd develop his photos in a darkroom in our basement, using chemicals that smelled so bad I bet everyone who lived in that house has never forgotten them.

Every now and then Dad would frame some up and show his stuff at local craft fairs. I could see how much this artistic expression meant to him, and how differently he lived when he was pursuing his passion. It was as if, in those moments, he was able to express something that he couldn't in the rest of his life. I think my dad also wanted to be a musician and play an instrument. Once, he told me he had drawn piano keys on a long piece of paper in an effort to learn how to play while he was growing up.

Outside of his hobbies, Dad was a quiet and kind man who loved reading, listening to CBC Radio, and playing all kinds of music. Mom and Dad would argue occasionally like any couple, but they seemed to have a loving and solid relationship for the most part, at least in my eyes. Dad could be resentful, and though he tried to keep those resentments to himself, Mom later told me that when they'd built up enough, he'd blow up over seemingly nothing. My mom would look at him and defuse the whole thing with cool precision. "You're not still mad at me about that, are you?" she'd say, and the whole thing would simmer down.

My parents were hard-working people, and they made sure that we were hard-working kids, at least when we weren't running around the yard driving them and each other crazy. There was always lots of housework to do, not least because of the nine-to-five routine our folks kept. We kids always had a schedule, a chore chart on the fridge, and knew what was expected of us. By and large we did our best to meet their expectations. And to help around the house we had Molly Salakin, a larger-than-life Ukrainian woman Mom hired. Molly helped keep the house tidy, and she'd be there when I got home from school, happy to make me a snack to tide me over until my parents got back from work. But Molly's snacks were not regular snacks. She would slather peanut butter and jelly on almost an entire loaf of bread, and she'd be visibly disappointed if you didn't make a sizable dent in her offering. She would make free-form desserts, mixing together marshmallows, Jell-O, pudding, and god knows what else in a gelatinous mound. And, as a Ukrainian, Easter was an especially important holiday for her; she'd lead all of us kids in painting eggs to mark the occasion. I always loved doing that.

Molly also had a habit of shopping for little gifts for me. They usually had a part missing or a visible defect—she bought them at the Salvation Army or other thrift stores—and I'm sorry to say I was most likely quite ungrateful in receiving her imperfect presents. But it never seemed to matter to Molly that I wasn't thrilled with her gifts. She'd pick me up and hug and kiss me and I'd be completely enveloped by her, and more than a little embarrassed at all the affection. Later, we had to let Molly go, as she developed an acute paranoia that led her to believe the guy reading the gas meter was a thief or a madman who was coming to find her. After receiving a frantic phone call saying someone outside was trying to kill her, Mom returned home to find Molly hiding in the closet with an axe, in complete terror. Turns out it was only the meter man, but that would be the end of her time with us. I still remember her fondly.

We were a late-sixties family through and through, and the politics and social upheaval influenced us as much as the music that was always playing. By the time I was four, John Kennedy, Bobby Kennedy, and Martin Luther King had all been assassinated. In America, the civil rights movement was in full swing, and protests against the Vietnam War were gaining traction. Folksingers, still popular in my house, had revolted against the social structures of the world through protest songs and actions, and then revolted again, against the rock 'n' roll that threatened to dethrone their particular brand of musical activism, as Dylan experienced in the mid-sixties when the folkies hated his electric turn. That movement was giving way to flower power, as the bloom of the beatniks and the boppers started to fade. In our house, though, there was room for it all. Woody Guthrie and Bob Dylan shared the turntable with Odetta and the Staples Singers. Simon and Garfunkel and Joni Mitchell were daily spins. Pete and Peggy Seeger made their case alongside the Supremes, who were . . . well, supreme. You couldn't fill your tank at the local Esso station or buy some milk at the Golden Mile Plaza without hearing them on the station or a store stereo, and they were in heavy rotation at 24th Street as well. In fact, I have a distant memory of lip-synching "Where Did Our Love Go?" using a lamp as a microphone while my parents laughed and laughed.

The words "no singing at the dinner table" were never heard in our house. Music was always around, and most of us were always singing along. I can still remember whole lyrics from the records I heard back then, and today, when I think of those songs, I will often ask Siri or Alexa to play them and I immediately get lost in the memory the music conjures. Music and memory. It's like kicking up the dust in a lovely forgotten room. Sometimes Cathy's room, listening to Desmond Dekker on her little plastic record player.

My parents subscribed to *Sing Out!*, a quarterly magazine about all things folk music, and you would always find copies piled around our living room. Looking back, it's probably how my folks were able to keep up with the scene as well as they did. They'd hear some folk music on the radio, of course, but my parents had a deep knowledge, and were always tuned in to the latest thing—and back then, *Sing Out!* would have been the best way to know what was coming up. They'd hear about whatever was new and hip, and soon enough it would make it to our house. In fact, *Sing Out!* might be to blame for how depressed I got whenever my parents put Leonard Cohen on the turntable. In the summer 1967 issue, the magazine featured not one but two articles on Mr. Cohen's particular brand of Montreal misery—one written by Buffy Sainte-Marie, which would have given him instant cred in those days—and even published the lyrics to "Suzanne." I now recognize the man's great talents, but to this day I get sort of melancholy when I hear him sing certain older songs from his canon, a long-held remnant of my childhood exposure. In fact, the only thing I found more depressing as a kid was the dreaded theme song to *Coronation Street*, which I'd only hear if I was faking being sick so I could stay home from school and watch TV. Back in those days there were only three channels in Saskatchewan, so when you heard the sad-sack trumpet start up, you knew the next half-hour was totally ruined! Bring on *The Flintstones* or *Get Smart*!

When we weren't at home singing along to records, we were outside. We'd take trips to the country all the time when I was little. These were free and easy days that my parents and all of us kids really loved. In summer, our destination was usually the Qu'Appelle or Lumsden Valley, a short drive north of Regina, where we'd all go pick chokecherries so that Dad could make his bitter homemade wine and Mom could make her chokecherry jam. It is a beautiful place, a rare piece of actual topography sinking down from the endless flat of the plains. We'd take a picnic and spend the whole day wandering the cactus-covered hills, looking for deer. Sometimes you'd come over a crest and see dozens of them running through the valley below, jumping fence posts and frolicking about.

Sometimes, on summer nights, our parents would say "hey, let's all jump in the car." We'd go to Dairy Queen (banana split for me!) and drive to the outskirts of Regina, deep into the countryside, then turn around and drive back into town. If you got far enough out, you could see the whole town laid out, lights popping up like stars from the endless prairie and then receding. If we'd driven to the east, we'd head back with the sun setting behind Regina. You could see the radio towers standing tall, blinking their little red lights. Even then,

I felt a romantic pull towards them, transmitting that magical thing that would be most precious in my life . . . music.

All in all, I was lucky. It was a pretty great way to grow up—loving parents, siblings to look up to, music in the air, and nature all around. It was typical, but in the nicest way. I played with my siblings and cousins and kids in the neighbourhood. I caused a bit of trouble from time to time, once disappearing completely in a little red plastic foot-to-floor fire truck my parents bought me. After some searching, Mom found me three or four blocks away, enjoying my first sweet taste of life on the road, away from everything.

When I was five or so, we finally settled at 2824 24th Avenue, where I spent the rest of my Regina childhood playing with slot cars and model trains and spending countless hours detailing a Canadian National Railway set I got for Christmas with little homemade trees and mountains made from stuff from the hobby store. In my little room, which was upstairs in the front left of our house, looking out to 24th Street, I would play with tiny paratrooper action figures you could buy for ten cents, the kind where you could ball up the parachute attached to their back then toss them and they would fly. I'd throw them out of my window and watch them gracefully float away towards whatever their future held. Mom bought me a book with instructions for making elaborate paper airplanes and helicopters, and I'd throw those too. When the wind was right, I'd open my window as wide as I could, angle myself seated on the sill, and toss whatever beautiful folded creation I'd made into the great blue sky outside. I'd watch it fly away, held aloft on the summer breeze, and dream of doing so myself one day.

CHAPTER TWO

ARMY OF HOPEFULS

MY MOM GREW UP in a BC mountain town called Hope—an optimistically named spot that is genuinely beautiful, at least when it's not mired in fog and rain. An old British Columbia logging town, it is a two-hour drive from Vancouver and was a frequent destination for our family's summer vacations. We'd load up our trusty dark-green International Harvester Travelall and blast tunes across the prairie, heading towards the dark and moody woods of BC. We'd all sing to hits by the Supremes, of course, but we'd also be wailing along to the Jackson 5. I remember being about eight years old, crammed in the family car, marvelling at Harry Nilsson's bizarre "The Lime in the

Coconut" or the lilting banjo in "Sweet City Woman" by Calgary's own the Stampeders.

In Hope, we'd visit with my grandparents on my mom's side, and it was always a memorable time. This was partly because they owned and operated a kind of general store called Buck's Confectionary, which sold penny candy and ice cream, and was thus a dream destination for any seven-year-old kid. And partly because of my grandfather, Joe Buck, born Bokinatz, whose father's father hailed from the Serbian town of Farkaždin, just north of Belgrade. Like many, Joe would shorten and change his Serbian last name to assimilate, but he did not change his demeanour, which was larger than life, but sadly not always in the best way. Later, the family would quietly chuckle that his chosen family name was shared by Jon Voight's drifter/gigolo character in the classic 1969 movie *Midnight Cowboy*!

My grandfather was a domineering and generally grumpy man whose foul moods were somewhat balanced by the warm, wonderful, and incredibly good-natured Grandma Kay. It always struck me as kind of funny to imagine my cranky, brooding Grandpa Joe angrily slinging ice cream to a bunch of yammering kids. To this very day I keep one of the metal scoops from Buck's Confectionary to remember this unlikely operation; it's in a kitchen drawer to the right of the dishwasher, and we still use it all the time. While the memory of lots of candy looms large in my mind, my mom reminded me that the store sold other, more practical things too. It had a meat counter, and was well-stocked with cheese, bread, canned goods, and everything else you might need for life in a small town. It was the sort of place where, as once happened to Grandpa Joe, you might look up from your paperwork to see a bear on the back porch.

Joe and Kay bought the general store in 1947. The family—including my mom, her sister Arlene, and her brother Doug, who would later prove a formative figure in my musical life—lived in the back of the store. My grandfather's perpetually gruff ways dominated the family but were known to the wider community too. My mom liked to tell stories of customers lingering outside the shop until Kay took over the counter from Joe, so that they could have a more pleasant shopping experience. Joe loved to drive his prized Mercury a little too fast from time to time, and he found himself in occasional conversation with the local police, who tried their best to discourage this habit. "Not again, Joe," they'd say, and my grandfather would offer a grumpy nod of assent, only to find himself in the same predicament the next week. My mom recalled one memorable drive when they ended up with two wheels hanging off a cliff. Joe's particular brand of cantankerous masculinity had a big effect on Mom, and I always understood that her incredible feminist strength was, in some part at least, a reaction against her dad's old-world macho dominance.

Growing up in Hope shaped my mom in other ways too, especially in her early awareness of the racism she would witness towards the Indigenous communities in the area, on the Ohamil and Chawathil reserves. She spent a lot of her time in the town's cafés, soaking up the early sounds of the folk music that would later come to dominate our house, and my early childhood. Also, it was in Hope that Mom had a favourite math and science teacher named Colin Robertson, who would later lend his first name to yours truly.

Despite the literal and figurative clouds that hung over the place, I remember my times in Hope with great warmth. It's a truly stunning place, and I think those early trips, along with others made to BC, shaped part of my own desire to live in that province, which I've now called home for more than forty years. And those summer trips were full of another thing precious in my young life: time with our extended family, especially my cousins in the Konrad family.

The Konrads were named for my aunt Arlene's husband, Pete Konrad, a native of Hope, a rough-and-tumble lumberjack with a kind face and big ears who was as friendly as he was rough around the edges. I really liked Pete. Once, when I was around ten, he gave me a ride from Regina to Calgary to visit a friend of mine who had moved there. He'd have been going on to Hope after that, and I remember him smoking about two packs of cigarettes in his land boat of a car with the windows rolled up as we rolled across the plains. At one point I remember leaning over to ask him why he smoked so much, and although I'm sure he said something polite enough, I laugh to imagine what he probably wanted to say to the annoying kid riding shotgun. Generally, we got along great. A few years after that drive, he was tragically killed in a logging accident when a tree unexpectedly fell on him.

During those early summers in Hope, and later in Regina, it was Pete and Arlene's kids—Doug, Kenny, and Lorna—whom we saw so much of. We were a big, close-knit group, and I still have pictures of us kids hanging out, usually with me wearing my ubiquitous little cowboy hat with a string under the chin, which I just loved back then. Our favourite pastime was playing baseball in the park right across from the store, cousins against cousins, and it was almost always a blast. I say almost because of the one time Kenny managed to bash me in the face with a baseball bat, resulting in a tearful trip to the doctor to tend to my nose. Come to think of it, Kenny may have reshaped my nose a few times over the years, happy to use a hockey stick when he didn't have a bat handy. Every time, it was an accident, of course, and all in good fun.

Family played a big role in our life at home in Regina too. We'd frequently get together at potlucks and parties, right through the late sixties and into the seventies. At some point after my early childhood trips to Hope, Arlene, having separated from Pete, moved herself and the kids to Regina, so we'd see a lot of those same cousins year round. Doug was the oldest—King Cousin to all, for sure, the one we all looked up to, an adventurous young man who travelled to India and hitchhiked through Europe. Most families have a King Cousin like this, an older one who charts a path for the rest of the kids to admire. Sadly, Doug died not too many years later, and that particular path was cut far too short. He was only thirty-four. My cousin Kenny, not far behind him in age, was the other big figure in my life at that point, and not just because of his wayward baseball bat.

Kenny was a hellraiser, but one who had some tenderness at his core. Once, when I was seven or so and very sick with whooping cough—I'd had an allergic reaction to penicillin as a baby and did not get the vaccine as a result—it was Kenny who unexpectedly turned up to comfort me. I had been upstairs in bed or tucked into the kitchen by the sink for at least a week with a garbage can between my knees, spewing long strings of phlegm up with my horrible unstoppable cough, when Kenny started to turn up daily, sitting beside me to read the entire *Wizard of Oz*, which of course made it all a little bit better.

The Konrads lived in a cool little two-storey hippie house, an old Craftsman with beautiful little stained glass windows at the top of the casings, and sometimes we'd end up there for rocking parties with family and friends. I recall stealing my first sips of wine from the kitchen at the tender age of ten, the adults otherwise occupied dancing or talking in the living room.

Sunday family dinner often featured our Konrad cousins, and the gatherings were big affairs. We'd convene at our place or theirs, and somebody would bring baked beans (usually my dad), somebody would make a big coleslaw. Both of those would be served in huge handmade pottery bowls, sometimes made by my uncle Doug or his then girlfriend Solvega. We'd have chicken and hamburgers going on the grill outside the back door, where the adults would be huddled on the stairs enjoying some Bohemian, the quintessential Saskatchewan beer in the little brown bottles. The kids would play tag or Frisbee or football, running around that yard that seemed so big then. Sometimes we'd head to Wascana Park when we needed space for an even bigger crew—watermelon and sunshine, the good times of summer, my bruised nose slowly healing from Kenny's wayward bat. In my mind, I can still smell the freshly cut grass.

We had other kinds of potlucks too, but those had to do with another important aspect of our family life. We were Quakers, and as such we were active with the local Society of Friends. That was, and still is, the the social conscience-driven, peace-loving, pacifist, "spiritual and political" religion that Mom and Dad had aligned our beliefs with, and that Mom in particular followed her whole life. At the time, it didn't occur to me to wonder how or why we were Quakers, but I would later learn that at the root of it all was a girlfriend of my mom's named Terry Padghan who had, years before, when they were teenagers in Hope, suggested that Mom should check out a Quaker meeting one day. By the time I came along, Quakerism was a fairly big part of our family life, and we'd often find ourselves gathering with our fellow Quakers for potlucks that were very much like our family ones.

In fact, Regina was a small enough place that a lot of the various "counterculture" groups, including hippies, peaceniks, union members, and even idealistic socialists and communists, often overlapped and bled together into one gathering. The late sixties and early seventies was an age of protests—anti–Vietnam War, of course, but also marches for women's rights or various rallies against environmental pollution, against nuclear weapons and power, political campaigns against the old guard and the Cold War–mongers. We were the children of a hopeful, maybe even idealistic, generation of parents, and our family's faith was a big part of that. In an era of war, it was political to be Quaker, because to be Quaker was to be pacifist. That our Quakerism also mapped so easily onto the Regina world of craft fairs and folk music concerts made it all even more natural. We were of the time, and the things that were important to us made it easy to fit into a big, welcoming, hippie-ish community of like-minded people—an army of hopefuls.

Quakerism also provided a certain structure to our family life. As little kids, we were brought up going to weekly meetings at the local YMCA. There would be an hour of silent sitting for the gathered Friends—the idea being that silence created space for individuals to commune with God—though we kids usually only made it for fifteen minutes or so before our fidgeting and giggling got in the way of anybody else's silent worship. We'd get sent outside the room to play shuffleboard and wait out the rest of the meeting. Twice a year our family would escape the confines of our insular Regina world and leave town for the bigger Quaker meetings. These trips were joyful for me. In spring, when Regina was still covered in a mix of snow, mud, and salt, we would drive through the mountains of Alberta and into the rugged and beautiful interior of British Columbia, where we'd have a three-day get-together with like-minded Quakers from all over Canada. We'd arrive in a little town called Sorrento, where the west coast spring would be in full bloom, cherry-blossomed trees and fresh mountain air everywhere. Sometimes we'd meet closer to home for quarterly gatherings at Lake Diefenbaker in Saskatchewan, and even once at Canada's oldest Benedictine monastery, St. Peter's Abbey, in a town called Muenster, also in our home province.

The adults would convene, presumably sorting out all sorts of important spiritual things that we were too young to know about, but for us kids meetings were basically chances to play epic games of hide-and-seek in unfamiliar surroundings. We would also explore everything and everywhere, opening every last door in the old monastery, or inspecting each room of whatever building we found ourselves in. At Lake Diefenbaker, we found a little trail going through the poplars that led to an old hunters' cabin, a dilapidated place full of tobacco tins from the 1930s. You can imagine how cool that would seem to a ten-year-old!

There were silent meetings, but we also went on beautiful mountain hikes, and the adults organized various activities—there were always initiatives like that, sponsoring war refugees, anti-nuclear rallies, or some other cause, usually three or four different ones on the go. That sort of activity, the social activist impulse, was crucial to the broader community and the Quaker tradition. Down the road, I'd bond over this shared experience with my good friend Bonnie Raitt, but that's a story for another day.

Despite the supportive environment of my family and the broader community, I did struggle with one particular thing as a kid. At some point in my young life, I became obsessed with life and death. What kind of cruel world, and cruel God, for that matter, would make life so great and then take it all away? I worried over this constantly, and eventually I started having terrifying nightmares. Some dreams would recur again and again. Often it would be me sitting in a chair in a solitary room with no doors and no windows and no possible way out. Nowadays that doesn't seem so scary, but when I was young it terrified me. As to what caused this unease, I can't be sure. Perhaps it was some of the difficult material that emerged though Quaker community activism—environmental issues and war and political unrest—or perhaps it was the fact that CBC news was always on in the kitchen, broadcasting waves of geopolitical bleakness and Cold War unease. But whatever the reason, around the age of six, I became a serious hypochondriac. I became convinced again and again that I had severe cancer. I'd picture my funeral and imagine my grieving parents expressing their deep regrets about not taking me seriously. "If only we'd listened to him when he said he thought he was dying," they'd say in these daydreams, as they threw clumps of dirt on my small coffin, "then our dear Colin would still be with us today!"

My parents tolerated my nightmares, graciously letting me crawl between them in bed to share the bad news of my latest self-diagnosis. I came down with eye cancer, foot cancer, tongue cancer, earlobe cancer, face cancer. I can laugh about this now, but at the time it was deadly serious. Lights out for little Colin, no doubt in my mind. And it must have been hard on them; even if they thought my worries were misplaced, it's still difficult to see your kid suffering. My parents would load me up for the cross-town trip to the doctor—the only thing that stopped my worrying—and I really appreciated that. It was a fairly frequent trip, however. Besides the doctor, who told me again and again that I did not have cancer of the nose, or whatever else I was fearing, only Mom could make things better. Her strength and optimism have been a major force in my life. "Colin," she would say after one of my freak-outs, "the human body is an amazing thing. Look at what it can do. Look what nature does. It is designed to work." That always made me feel better, at least until my next meltdown.

In a sense, something of that worry would stay with me my whole life. To this day, anxiety can grip me out of the blue, though it's all a lot better than when I was young. But I suppose it has its virtues, too. As Pete Seeger used to say, "It takes a worried man to sing a worried song." And I'd end up singing a lot of those.

Next to music, the biggest shared joy in our family was the great outdoors, and we spent as much time as possible outside. Those family trips to the Qu'Appelle and Lumsden Valley were hallmarks of my childhood, but we undertook grander adventures as well. Sometimes we'd head to the Cypress Hills, a spot down in the southwestern corner of the province, near the Alberta border, where American wolf hunters had attacked a Nakoda First Nation camp in a horrific massacre in 1873. It's the highest point between the Appalachians and the Rocky Mountains, and was uniquely spared by the little ice age ten thousand years ago—you can see for miles and miles.

We also loved to camp, and spent a lot of vacation time up in northern Saskatchewan at Waskesiu Lake, Doré Lake, Beaupré Creek, and other spots. I have many fond memories of campfires and the endless mossy green of the woods. I was absolutely in love with that earthy smell of wet pine and the general feel of the wilderness up there. I've never seen more moose and bear than we did in those days. If you found just about any sizable body of water up above the tree line, you'd most likely find a moose if you looked close enough.

I learned to "swim" at a place called Candle Lake—I use quotes because I distinctly remember misrepresenting the whole thing to my parents as I put my hands on the lake bottom in the shallows and kicked my legs frantically behind me to make it look as though I was really swimming. Oh, Colin . . . why'd you lie? My parents watched on and placated me with false flattery.

My dad loved fishing, so that was a major activity during many of our camping trips. I caught my very first fish in Wood Buffalo National Park, right on the cusp of where Saskatchewan becomes Manitoba. When I was seven or eight, my parents bought me a kid's fishing set, the sort of thing you might buy today at the dollar store. It had a little reel and rod, and I went to this big lake there and cast my spoon in the water. I caught a fish, but despite being the son of an accomplished angler, I somehow, in my panic, forgot that you were supposed to reel it in. So I started walking, keeping the line tight by slowly backing away from the beach towards the tackle store. Soon, my fish emerged in the distance as I dragged it onto the shore, and I threw down my gear to secure my first catch from the sand.

Often my dad would take us to a place south of Doré Lake called Beaupré Creek for a week at a time to catch the hard-fighting but super-bony northern pike. We would run up and down the trails to find the best fishing spots on the creek. My siblings and I would also make cool boats out of random planks of wood we found scattered about and then decorate them with animal skulls, moss, rocks, and anything else we could find lying around. We'd then launch the boats downstream and run along the mossy paths to see whose would win the race before they were all toppled by a waterfall. Big fun indeed.

In 1972, the summer I turned eight, we took the first of two monumental family trips, this one to visit an old friend of Mom's who lived near Cody, Wyoming, who ran a kind of animal rescue there. She commanded a full-on menagerie. There was a Doberman pinscher who had suffered some sort of brain deterioration, which made him even more terrifying than he would normally be. A blind, decrepit poodle roamed the house, and you'd hear it banging into the walls in the middle of the night. An old, retired racehorse lived there too, which was amazing for us kids; I have a photo of all of us on that horse, and I remember sitting on it and thinking, "Here I am in Wyoming sitting on a horse and this is just *so cool*." A talking parrot completed the scene, and we'd hear him squawking away all day. On that same trip we toured Yellowstone, and went all through northern Montana. Then we made it to Portland, Oregon, and came back up the west coast. At one stop we all tried to taste big, fat oysters from a jar. I recall the unanimous kid verdict was "Gross, Mom!"

We ended up in Tofino, which was basically a hippie camp settlement back then. There must have been three hundred tents on the beach flying Canadian flags, the skull and crossbones, and other flags of various colours that would allow you to distinguish your camping spot from someone else's on the crowded beach. We stayed there for a few days, exploring and taking in the scene. Cathy and I took some starfish out of the water and brought them back to our campsite.

We were excited to show off our great discovery, only to realize that, on account of us having removed them from their habitat, they'd died. We felt so guilty! My psychic wound was soon matched by a physical one—karma perhaps. We had a camp lantern, the kind with a filament, and I think we must have forgotten to turn it off one day. We got back to camp one afternoon and I put my hand right on it, burning it very badly. I had a big pus-bubble blister on my hand for weeks. It was an unforgettable trip, and it would be a few years before we attempted anything quite so epic again.

For the second big family journey, we went all the way to Ottawa. In my mind, it isn't as vivid, but one hilarious image endures: a photo we took of the whole family crossing Ottawa's Abbey Road, pretending we were a lesser, Ontarian version of the Beatles.

My birthday is in August, and so it often fell during one of our summer trips. I can't say a lot of planning went into the celebrations—there was so much organization already under way just to keep all of us kids in line on the road—but the occasion never went unmarked. Somewhere on the back roads of BC or Alberta or Montana, wherever we happened to be, our International Harvester would glide into a parking lot at a Safeway or a gas station restaurant, like the old Voyageur restaurants that were attached to Esso stations in Canada back then. A cake would be procured, a few candles lit, and that night, at whatever campsite we happened to have settled in, I'd turn six or seven or eight. It was a gift, growing up like that, surrounded by family in the vast wildernesses of western North America.

When I finally started going to school, I found that I was always a lot less interested in what was happening in class than I was in the endlessly intriguing sounds that emerged from the family stereo, or the bracing, unforgettable smell of the pine trees that surrounded whatever campground we had been at that summer. My parents had to drag me kicking and screaming, quite literally, to kindergarten, though, perhaps predictably, I ended up having a crush on my teacher. Overall, my early academic years were pretty forgettable, aside from attending a little hippie daycare where I'd meet Kirsten Cameron, a friend for life whose family would later be instrumental in my musical development. I also made other friends in the neighbourhood, and around the age of six or seven I had an especially tight bond with two of my neighbours and classmates, Brad and Brent.

Brad, Brent, and I weren't just buddies. We were the Eagle Gang, sworn allies and friends forever. Brad lived a block away from us, but his family also had a farm close to Regina and an actual ranch in the Qu'Appelle Valley. Sometimes the three of us would go there. It mostly just housed cows, but we'd take BB guns and try to shoot magpies and gophers. Even then, I didn't want to kill anything, so I would be sure never to hit one.

At one point, as often happens in groups of little kids who have sworn eternal loyalty to each other, something broke up the band. My fellow Eagle Gang members became convinced that I'd betrayed them in some way (for the record, I must note that I had done no such thing). Despite my protestations, the message was clear: "You've told the secrets of the Eagle Gang, and now you're going to pay." I couldn't believe it. My best friends were threatening to beat me up after school as I walked home!

But I had an idea. In the boys' bathroom, I went up to some older students and told them that two kids in my grade were going to try to beat me up after school at the south fence. Would they help me? Perhaps I was an extraordinarily persuasive person, or perhaps one should never underestimate the blood lust of fifth-graders. Whatever the reason, they agreed to help me, and basically the whole older grade showed up after school and all of a sudden my fellow Eagle Gang members were under serious threat themselves, getting whaled by dozens of big kids. I had used my powers to the wrong end, and I once again felt an immediate wave of guilt. I ran across the schoolyard, making a beeline for my house, only to find my uncle Doug.

"Uncle Doug," I yelled, "they're killing my friends! You gotta help!"

Uncle Doug tore across the road, screaming at the brawling boys. Uncle Doug is a softie at heart, but that day he showed he was also my mean Grandpa Joe's son. He scattered the kids and saved my friends, and while the bond of the Eagle Gang was never quite as unshakable again, Brad, Brent, and I stayed friends for at least a few years after that, but then we lost touch the way you do sometimes with people in your life.

When I was five years old, my parents gave me my first record, Cat Stevens's *Tea for the Tillerman*, and I played it constantly. Like I said, music was everywhere growing up—on the handmade stereo my dad built at our house, blasting out of the windows of random passing cars, playing in the background at the grocery store or gas station. But owning my very own album, actually holding this magic black disc that made sound when you put it on the turntable . . . that was a special thing. And that connection just got deeper as my musical tastes started to expand, thanks to two key figures: Uncle Doug, saviour of the Eagle Gang, and my brother Robbie.

Uncle Doug is an incredible guy, and he and I have always had a special relationship. When I was growing up, he'd settled in Regina alongside his sisters—my mom, Joyce, and Aunt Arlene. He was the baby of the family, and always relished the role of cool uncle. In some ways, even in his early eighties, I think he still relishes it today. Like his sisters, he was also a social worker and part of that same Regina counterculture. He wore his hair a bit long, often in a ponytail, and sometimes he could be found hanging around the house wearing that old-timey kind of underwear where the whole thing is one big suit with a buttoned hatch in the butt. He was a bit of a ladies' man, a hippie on the go, and he drove a cherry-red Austin Mini convertible with flower decals. Nice! He'd turn up at our house and say, "Colin, we're going to the beach!" Or "Colin, we're going for ice cream! Hop in the car!" Which I would, with delight. And Doug was funny—*really* funny. Fart jokes for miles. Every year, he'd send out a Christmas card that would feature him in some hilarious pose. One year he wore a scuba mask, his face shoved into an aquarium. Years later, when my first record came out, his Christmas card featured him in full Hare Krishna garb, proudly standing in front of a downtown Vancouver record store that was plastered with posters advertising my album.

Later, in my teens, Doug would have a lot of social crossover with some of the people I played with in my earliest days as a musician, but at this point his role in my musical life was more like that of a guide. He loved the same stuff my parents did, of course, and I can remember Crosby, Stills, Nash, and Young harmonizing from his car speakers with clarity. But his tastes also roamed more widely. He loved the Chieftains and Little Feat and Cream, absolutely, but also unexpected, worldly music. He was obsessed, for instance, with Alan Stivell, the French-born Celtic harpist. It was through Doug that my musical horizons widened. When I was about ten, Doug came over with a very special gift: a B.B. King songbook that came with an instructional 45 record that you could pull out of the book and play on the stereo. It goes without saying that it pretty much blew my mind, and pointed me on a very particular path.

Around the same time, Robbie, seven years older than me, was living in the basement of the 24th Street house. To little me, it might as well have been a superhero's secret compound. Sometimes marijuana smoke would billow out of the door when it was opened, much to my parents' annoyance, but what I was captivated by were the sounds that emanated from his dungeon lair. Robbie loved Jimi Hendrix and Santana, and I was thrilled by the soaring guitar tones. Alvin Lee's guitar on "Ten Years Later," another Robbie fave, stood out too. My brother took inspiration from his heroes and picked up the guitar himself. He played an old, heavy, and probably not very good Fender acoustic, and though he lived downstairs, the guitar would often be lying around the house so that he could play it when he ventured out of his subterranean realm.

At the time, Robbie was fixated on the first, self-titled record by Hot Tuna, the great blues group that emerged from Jefferson Airplane and featured Jorma Kaukonen and Jack Casady. That album, with its hazy blue-and-red cover, was in frequent rotation in the basement. It's a live album of acoustic blues, and Robbie learned guitar by playing along to the record. I wouldn't really hear the album, which must have stayed downstairs, but instead I'd hear Robbie's renditions of those songs. One really stood out—the Hot Tuna version of "Death Don't Have No Mercy," the Reverend Gary Davis song that had been on his album *Harlem Street Singer* a decade or so before. It has this great opening riff, and Robbie would sit around the living room or the dining room or wherever he pleased, banging it out. He played the song so much it was burned in my mind, even though I'd probably never even heard the Hot Tuna version outside of muffled sounds emerging through the floorboards.

One day, when I was about eight and nobody was around, I picked up Robbie's guitar and sat down. I held it in my hands and placed it the way Robbie did, ready to strum. But it didn't feel right. Robbie is a leftie, and I'm right-handed, and so the whole thing was topsy-turvy, with the high E string at the top of the fretboard. I didn't know it at the time, but Jimi Hendrix had faced the same problem. He solved it by playing a right-handed guitar strung upside down, but that was not an option available to me that day in our Regina living room.

Instead, I laid the guitar on its back in my lap, so I could play the low strings more easily, fretting the notes with my thumb. With Robbie's version of Hot Tuna's version of Gary Davis's immortal blues running through my mind, I picked the tune out, then picked it out again. It was hard to hold the strings down—they were heavy, I was playing it wrong, and I struggled. But that didn't matter. The minute I felt that connection, those notes emerging from the magic combination of wood and steel and my own effort, something clicked into place.

CHAPTER THREE

TROUBADOUR IN THE MAKING

I KEPT BANGING AWAY on that lefty guitar that I would hold face up on my lap for a whole year, until a better one emerged—a blond Norman acoustic, made in Quebec, which my other brother had brought into the house when I was nine or ten. It was right-handed, improving things dramatically for me, since I could actually play it as intended. I believe it was with that guitar that I made my first recording, using a big square cassette tape recorder like you'd find in an office at the time. Amidst the avocado-tint tile of our downstairs bathroom, just off the front foyer, I taped myself playing slide and singing Elmore James's famous "Dust My Broom." I remember thinking it didn't sound bad at all, thanks to the natural reverb you sometimes find in bathrooms!

Not long after that, my parents both suggested that perhaps it was time I took some private guitar lessons so I could learn some music theory, chord structure, and scales. Were my parents genuinely supportive of my new passion? Absolutely. Were they also happy about the prospect of the continuous noise they had to overhear all day from my bedroom improving a little bit? Almost certainly. I appreciated the encouragement, but I wasn't super keen on turning the one thing I loved completely into something as tawdry and distasteful as a *class*. I had to put up with that all day at Argyle Elementary School, the prison where I was enduring grade five, but my parents were enthusiastically persistent, and in the end I said I would give music lessons a shot. And so it was that I began lessons every Saturday morning at a downtown music store called Arcade Music Centre.

The store was on Scarth Street, on a block recently upgraded into an open-air shopping promenade, anchored by a historic post office and with some beautiful old buildings lining either side of it. I'd take the city bus downtown, walk around and check out the records and tapes in Kelly's Stereo Mart, then head to the second floor of the music shop, where the lessons were held. On the way upstairs I'd linger over the rows of electric guitars for sale, dreaming of one day owning one. My first true love? A clear Plexiglas guitar. I couldn't tell you why, except that it looked pretty cool. Happily for me, I also lusted over a little sunburst Epiphone ET-275, which, after some convincing, my parents bought for me. I'd stand among the instruments each week, soaking up the sweet chemical smell of nitrocellulose coming from their newly dried finishes. To this day, that particular smell sends me right back to Scarth Street.

My teacher started me with major scales and basic notation—scales that I still know to this day! I would learn to play them up and down the neck, and then I'd be sent home with exercises and written notes to help with my practice. I really did try to do my homework, but usually I'd end up putting on a Steve Miller record, or Fleetwood Mac's early, pre–Stevie and Lindsey, bluesy stuff. I'd drop the needle again and again on a particular part of a song, playing along until I could get close enough to the phrasing. It was a great way to learn licks, even if I disappointed my teacher a bit come Saturday mornings. The electric guitar's thinner strings allowed me to bend notes far more easily than on an acoustic, and I could even play bar chords, the sort of things that filled the popular songs of the day, like Lynyrd Skynyrd's "Sweet Home Alabama" or the Doobie Brothers' "China Grove" or the languid opening of "Smoke on the Water." My folks worked all day, and school was very close to our house, so I could always walk the short distance home and wail away without disturbing them or the neighbours.

In addition to that sweet-smelling Epiphone, my parents soon bought me a second-hand Vagabond amplifier that they found in a newspaper classified ad. Another sensory discovery: the peculiar and irresistible smell of hot tubes cooking on a cranked amp. It was made by a Winnipeg company called Garnet, which turned out great-sounding but inexpensive amps to be sold under different brand names at department stores like Eaton's or Sears. The bottom speaker cone on mine was ripped, which gave it a distinctive natural growl when the amp was turned up loud; it produced a sound you might otherwise get from an overdrive pedal, the same sound that ran through my head again and again as I played "China Grove" on the turntable in my mind. I could make that sound now! Or something close enough to it. It's an incredible thing to be able to do, and I still marvel over the fact that, with a bit of practice, a sound you *hear* in your head can become a sound you *make*.

Thanks to my parents and the booming music scene in Regina growing out of the Regina Folk Guild and its annual festival, I was soon finding inspiration on stages big and small around town. At the Fourth Dimension in the River Heights Shopping Centre, I would sometimes sit right on the floor a few feet from the performers and watch their hands and learn from their crowd banter. The Folk Guild branched out, too—one week you'd hear Celtic fiddle tunes and sea shanties and the next it would be straight-ahead blues or original folk music. Add in some field hollers and gospel music, a bit of country and bluegrass, and you can see how the musical seeds were being sown in me slowly but surely.

We'd go to these concerts as a family, or sometimes Mom, Dad, and I would go alone. They knew how much it thrilled me to see these performers, and they were always happy to encourage that interest. We would even go out and see live jazz once in a while, and I must confess that the music was a complete mystery to me. It left me somewhat emotionally cold as a kid. I love jazz now, but at the time I was baffled by the way the players would improvise their solos over such varied and quick chord changes. It felt like a kind of magic I might never quite understand.

Yes, our little prairie town had a thriving music scene and art scene, and one that supported itself. Each year there would be the annual Regina arts and craft fairs, the ones where my dad would sometimes sell his photographs, and everyone would gather, the potters and the painters and the musicians and the hippies and the Quakers. It was at those fairs where I'd meet some of the people who'd turn out to be crucial figures in my musical education, my informal teachers and mentors. When musicians would come through and play the Guild coffee house, there would often be a house party afterward, hosted by someone in the scene. A Folk Guild member would volunteer his or her address after the show and local musicians and hangers-on would turn up until all hours, and a jam would inevitably ensue. We went to parties like that so often that even a young kid like me got comfortable enough to grab a guitar and join in as part of a big late night musical party. It was probably at one of these gatherings that I first played the mandolin, an instrument I'd soon become obsessed with—so much so that it would even dethrone the guitar for a few years in my personal pantheon of instruments. On those nights the wine and beer would flow freely, but in those days that didn't interest me; I was there for one thing and one thing only. Candles would be lit and big laughs would mix with the music. Everybody in attendance at those late night parties who could play would play, and everybody else would sing along, and together we would make that particular kind of magic happen. I loved every second of it.

Much of the action would take place at the annual folk festival itself, when everything was super-sized. Musicians would come from all over the world, and for three days they'd play—workshops all afternoon and full concerts at night. Workshops would take place in classrooms at the old Regina College by Wascana Lake (Sea Shanties from 3:30 to 4:30 p.m. in room 132!), and in the evenings the big shows would be held in Darke Hall. For those three days it felt as if Regina was the centre of the musical world. Or at least it did until we started our annual trips to Winnipeg for their new folk festival, which quickly became an even bigger deal. Starting in the summer of 1975, we'd pack up the trusty International Harvester and head east for the festival, which had just begun the year before. Over the years, I'd see countless legends there: Pete Seeger, Elizabeth Cotten, Johnny Shines, Roosevelt Sykes, Doc Watson, Stan Rogers, Stéphane Grappelli, the Red Clay Ramblers, John Goodman, Dave Van Ronk, and, among many others, John Hammond, who would become one of my all-time favourites.

The way John Hammond could play the overblown harmonica notes on the rack while rhythmically beating his National into a frenzy really blew me away. Down the road, at the age of sixteen, I'd be invited to introduce him at a show in Regina, and I'd be brave enough to ask him if he'd meet me for breakfast so I could ask him some questions about the music business. He graciously agreed, and kindly met me at his downtown hotel restaurant, where he nursed a coffee and smoked Pall Malls as I breathlessly praised him and peppered him with all kinds of questions. He did kindly ask at that time if we could avoid talking about his famous producer father, John Hammond Senior, which I must confess left me a little baffled in the moment. I later learned that a deep divide had separated the two when John Jr. embraced the blues as his chosen idiom, somehow displeasing his famous dad. In 1987, I'd run into John Jr. at Austin's seventh annual Riverfest, and later still I'd end up playing mandolin with him on a Mississippi Sheiks song, both on record and live on stage right here in Vancouver. But that's a story for another day.

Each year, we'd go to Winnipeg to hear bluegrass, authentic delta blues, and singer-songwriters performing their new music. It was a treasure trove, a who's who of modern folk and blues and world music. We'd soak up the sounds with a fervour, we'd buy the records of the acts we liked the best at the merch booths, and then we'd bring it all home to Saskatchewan, where I'd cherish the festival's memories and the music we'd returned with. What a way to learn and keep wanting to learn. A few years later I'd have one of my first professional gigs there, an afternoon workshop slot with my blues duo, the Hoodoo Men. And some years after that, I'd headline the main stage. But I had a bit more to experience before that.

Those festivals inspired me deeply, but some of the people I met at them made an even bigger impact, two in particular. The first was a rowdy, passionate, charismatic Saskatchewan blues player named Dave McLean—known to all in the area as Big Dave McLean. Dave would usually be performing, along with his brother Jim, everything from straight blues to gospel. They were a bit less folksy than some of their festival mates, and I loved them for it. I was never a shy kid, and especially when playing live; whatever reticence I might have had about performing in public had long ago burned off at the post-concert house parties where I was learning traditional Celtic music and having a blast. It was this confidence that would somehow find me backstage at one of Dave's festival shows when I was about ten years old. I asked him if he could show me how to play a simple blues turnaround that I'd seen him play on the guitar earlier that day. He could have told me to get out of there, made up a quick excuse, or perhaps just asked me to leave him alone. But that isn't Dave. To this day he's still an encouraging, inspiring force for musicians all around the country. He took me over to his guitar case, pulled out his instrument, and taught me the part on the spot, backstage. A lifelong friendship was forged then and there, though we couldn't possibly have known it at the time.

The other key figure I met in those days—another lifelong friend, and a frequent collaborator to this day—was Colin Linden. Colin and I met at the Regina Folk Festival, where I would often volunteer at a health food snack booth on site. For me, it was a way to be close to the action, and I'd bring along my guitar, noodling through my shift to pass the time. One day I was playing and a cherubic young man of about sixteen walked up to the booth, looking for a coffee and a cookie. I was lost in whatever song I was playing, and eventually he offered a comment. "You're sounding pretty good there!" Once I tuned back in and started getting his order together, I realized who he was, and I was over the moon. Colin was the talk of the festival at the time. His incredibly young age and his encyclopedic knowledge and mastery of all kinds of blues and ragtime finger-picking styles had fast made him a local folk music celebrity. It was said that he'd once met Howlin' Wolf, and he was known to play bass lines with his nose while he picked the melody with his fingers. He was three years older than me, but soon enough we got talking about both being Colins, and we became fast friends. He would go on to become one of the most important figures in my musical life, and I'd draw on his encyclopedic knowledge of music and natural-born talent across my career. We have been through everything over so many years, we're still friends, and at the time of this writing we have made six records together along the way.

When I was about thirteen, my parents made another major investment in my musical future in the form of a custom instrument commissioned from Regina luthier Peter Sawchyn. Peter was just starting out in what would become a long, storied career of making fine instruments for acoustic players of all kinds. I can't remember if it was my mom's or my dad's idea, but I do remember going to Peter's incredible workshop and seeing how that particular alchemy happened, how rough sheets of wood were sanded, shaped, and carved into these beautiful guitars; how each one's shape was built for a certain sound; and how the finest adjustments in the bracing inside the body could make or break the whole thing. I remember seeing the figure-eight outline of what would become my guitar hanging from the ceiling of his workshop after it was shaped, and the intricate way a rosette was made from long strands of coloured wood glued together in patterns and then sliced like bread to encircle and adorn the sound hole. The end result was amazing: a D-18-style dreadnought with a beautiful abalone bird-and-butterfly inlay on the headstock. Even more amazing, I own it to this day. Despite a brief separation, which I'll come back to, it's been with me throughout my career, and hangs on the wall of my living room as I write these words. In fact, it might be time to go grab it and play a tune or two . . .

While I was becoming more steeped in folk and other acoustic music, I was yearning to play more modern rock 'n' roll with kids my own age. That began to happen thanks to a few of my classmates—David and Joel Silverman, who were my closest friends in my early teens, after things cooled with my fellow Eagle Gang members Brad and Brent. For once I found myself bashing away on instruments with my peers instead of providing accompaniment for the folkie social set my parents had brought me into. While I'd loved my time on the mandolin, it was good to be back on an electric guitar, where I could play along to my records or the radio. Steve Miller was huge at the time, and of course Santana. David and Joel's family owned a big north-end furniture store called George Silverman's Furniture Warehouse, and they had a cool house I loved hanging out at, with an ideally situated garage that had doors opening up onto a big, undeveloped field across from our school's playground.

David, Joel, and I would get out of class, go straight to their place, open the garage doors, turn on David's amplifier, and crank out some of the hits of the day. The Doobie Brothers were favourites there, too, especially "Takin' It to the Streets," which is a great song to play when you're finding your feet on electric guitar. David's parents had bought him a white 1976 Fender Stratocaster that I was intensely jealous of. Don't get me wrong, I loved my little sunburst Epiphone, but there was something about the Strat—the elegant lines of it, the shape of it.

We weren't a band, not really. We were a people-summoning machine. As soon as the garage doors opened and the power chords rang out, kids would stop by to listen. And, most notably, girls. Our school was home to an incredible number of them. They hailed from all over, neighbourhoods near and far, and the three of us couldn't get enough of that attention. We didn't play music for the love of it, though we did love it. We didn't play music for the camaraderie in creating it, though that was nice too. No, we played music because we liked the girls, and, happily, the girls seemed to like us. We'd look out over the abandoned field as a small group of them drifted from the schoolyard towards the noise we were making, and it felt as though we were manifesting our wildest dreams, right there in the stubby grass. Later that year I'd have my first kiss with a girl from school named Linda in the loft above where the cars would park in that very garage, bringing a brand new obsession into focus. Oh, sweet life.

While my musical education was proceeding, my other education wasn't going as well. In grade five I had an amazing teacher named Mrs. McDonald, a kind and patient woman who listened to me and took my questions seriously, no matter how off-topic or bizarre they were. My questions were informed by CBC Radio and Quaker meetings, so they probably focused on anxiety about pollution and the environment. But sadly for me, there weren't any other Mrs. McDonalds at Argyle Elementary, and I struggled in all my classes thereafter. In grade six I had a teacher who was so mean and miserable that I won't name her here. It was the beginning of the end for me as far as conventional education was concerned. Grade six is such a heady time—innocent childlike curiosity giving way to sexual awakenings and school crushes as mischief becomes the order of the day. The TV series *Charlie's Angels* dominated our young minds, and we all carried combs in our back pockets to keep our hair fluffy and feathered, jerking our heads back habitually.

The teacher ruled over us all, and she seemed to relish the opportunity to embarrass anyone for anything. If she saw you with your shirt unbuttoned, she'd call out, "Oh, Mr. Man, how manly you are, let us see your chest hair!" *Heartless* is the word I'd use to describe her; she'd crush each of our tiny dreams in turn, all the while lecturing us about brushing our teeth with baking soda. Once, a local theatre company was auditioning school kids for a production of *Oliver!*, and the people putting it on heard I could sing, so they sought me out. I had the misfortune of overhearing the teacher in the hallway telling them I was not a very good student and that the play would only make me a worse one, so they shouldn't even consider casting me. I'd leave school just a few years later, never quite getting over the experience of being punched down by her.

All of that time, I took sanctuary, as kids have for generations, in the stories of J.R.R. Tolkien. By grade six I'd read *The Hobbit* and devoured *The Lord of the Rings*. I'd wake up early and spend some quality time with my friends in Middle Earth over a breakfast of toast with honey and tea in an earthenware mug. The grandeur of the story captivated me—the lore, the language, the passionate search for truth and goodness. And it dovetailed perfectly with what was going on in my life at the time, where the Folk Guild jams were introducing me to the kind of traditional music I felt sure would have been playing at a party in the Shire. It certainly was playing in our house while I ate my toast like a good little hobbit. Out of this confluence came a deep obsession with Celtic and other forms of traditional music. To this day I still have the cheap binder that served as my traditional fiddle songbook as a kid, on whose pages I wistfully illustrated pennywhistles, mandolins, and bodhrans in pencil. It holds lists of the keys and titles of the many Scottish, Irish, and Métis fiddle tunes I knew by heart.

Those Folk Guild parties started stretching deeper into the night as I got even more serious about playing with those gifted but older musicians in my early teen years. They welcomed me into their world. Some nights I'd be out until 5 a.m., gleefully strumming my mandolin, feeling like I was about to set off on a grand adventure to Mordor myself. I remember my dad saying to me that I was out partying too much. "Keep that up and you won't have any party left in you when you get older, Colin," he'd say. "I don't think that's really true, Dad," I'd offer in return, and I think it's fair to say I've been mostly proven right on that front. Mind you, I do think that the lifestyle of a musician can burn anyone out if they don't pace themselves to a degree. Endless hours of travelling and boredom between shows can take a toll.

Things at home were shifting then, too. With my older siblings having gone out into the world to make lives for themselves, our family felt smaller. Perhaps that's why I started to notice that things between my parents were changing too. There were little tensions that lingered, the sort of thing that, when I was younger, would have been laughed off by my mom or let go by my dad. There were eerie silences after I'd enter the room and a conversation or argument between them would be quickly hushed. My mom, ever gregarious and generally upbeat, and my dad, more introverted and prone to moods, were finding it harder and harder to keep their relationship in balance as the years went by. Once, I came down the stairs to find Mom on the couch, alone, crying. Another time, on a camping trip, they fought in front of us all. Dad was driving, and as his anger rose, so did our speed. Finally, Mom panicked and made him pull over and stop. Those moments rattled me, but when you're a kid you don't suspect the worst, or at least I didn't. You hope that discord like that is normal, and that your family will stay together forever.

One day, home alone at age twelve or so, I took it upon myself to clean the house. In the beginning, I mostly just tidied—I'd stack magazines that were scattered around a coffee table, or put books back on the shelf. I'd organize the kitchen, lining things up nicely, making sure everything looked crisp. And this earned me real praise from Mom and Dad. My parents would come home from work and say how wonderful it was to come back to such an orderly home. They loved it!

And I loved the praise, so I continued my work. I started clearing the table and dusting and putting random stuff away in storage. I got very into vacuuming; I was always fascinated by the rhythm and motion of it, and I loved the little headlight that was on our vacuum, so you could see the dust you were about to bust in the dark corners of the room. I liked the way the cord got sucked into the vacuum's bowels when you pressed the little lever. I even got into polishing the hardwood floors in the dining and living rooms, using one of those old machines where you hit the button and it kind of pulled you along the floor. Picture twelve-year-old Colin, home alone, blasting Steppenwolf and getting dragged around by a floor waxer. It was incredibly fun. Looking back now, it feels a bit more melancholy, and I wonder if my obsession with cleaning the house resulted in some way from the low-level instability in our family, if fixating on order and cleanliness was my way of offsetting the disorder I was starting to sense. I guess I'll never know. But at least the floors shined.

There was, however, one area of our home that was decidedly untidy, and the fault lay completely with me. Our family's dining room looked out at the backyard, and for years my seat was against the window, near the furnace vent. As a kid, I'd always hated peas and was none too pleased when they were served at mealtime. So, for years my peas would make their way off my plate and into the vent below my chair. I'd wait until no one was looking, then scrape them into the grate, where they'd go straight down the pipe and right into the furnace in the basement. One day I was minding my own business in the living room when I heard my dad yell out from the basement, "Colin! Get down here!" He called me back into the furnace room, and showed me the filter in the heater. Somehow it was covered with hundreds of dried peas! He asked if it was my doing, and I insisted it wasn't. Only now that the statute of limitations on pea prosecution has long since expired can I come clean. I'm lucky I didn't ruin the furnace!

Through these years, Mom and I stayed close. She was great about making sure we spent time together, and especially patient in indulging my many specific interests. A lot of these things were in line with the sorts of activities that were common in our Quaker community. I'd bug Mom to go to the Centre of the Arts, where we saw the blues great Taj Mahal a week after I turned twelve, and where we took in the gleeful melodies of a Gilbert and Sullivan show like *H.M.S. Pinafore*. But I had other curiosities too, especially when it came to the sorts of activities that were not as common in our hippie Quaker community—the kinds of things I'd hear about my friends' families doing, things that seemed wild, exotic, mysterious, almost illicit. Things like *bingo*.

"Mom," I'd say, "did you know there's a bingo night at the banquet hall at the Centre of the Arts? Not in the hall where the seats are, but below that, downstairs in the basement of the building, I hear they play bingo there, have you ever played bingo? What's it like to play bingo? Could *we* play bingo?" It probably took me a few weeks of nagging, but one night I got my wish—Mom finally acquiesced with an exasperated, "Okay! I'll take you to play bingo already!" I was over the moon, strutting through the venue, picking up our cards and daubers, then sitting down in total confusion amongst the profusion of hairsprayed perms and polyester pantsuits. The swirling sea of cigarette smoke rose from the half-full ashtrays amid the sweet smell of *eau de toilette*.

I got the hang of the game quickly enough, and I could see, lying before me, a long, glorious night of riches and fame. I was made for bingo, and soon enough everyone would see that. But something was wrong, and Mom suddenly put her head down on her folded arms, resting on the table. I asked her if she was okay, and she assured me she was, she just needed to rest for a second. She didn't feel well, she said, but not to worry, she'd be fine. All around us the noise of the hall continued, people finding precisely the sort of success I myself was destined for. I patted Mom's shoulders to comfort her and did a reasonable job of performing the role of good son, all the while keeping one eye on my card.

After another few minutes, she sat up straight, eyes bulging, and time seemed to hold still for what seemed like forever. I wasn't exactly sure what was happening, and then Mom reared back, bent forward, and puked all over the bingo cards, covering ours and everyone else's around us, simultaneously snuffing out a cigarette or two in the process. I was mortified for her, and for me. After that, we stuck to concerts. I'd learned that bingo was not a "Munn family" kind of thing.

So there I was, thirteen years old, playing music deep into the night with a revolving group of people who were significantly older than me, checking out shows with my parents, hitting the craft fairs, and obsessively playing and practising not just guitar, but mandolin.

Looking back, I had no idea how unusual this arrangement was; it didn't strike me as strange that I hung out mostly with adults, or that they always seemed to welcome me into their midst. In a sense, it wasn't weird at all, though I did have one older musician friend who pulled back a bit because he got worried that others might have the wrong idea about him hanging around with someone my age. But I think most people didn't give it a second thought—I think they saw me as a passionate kid who had a lot to offer creatively, and who was always trying to soak up anything, especially music, that he could. Which is why, when some of those same musicians and artists asked me and my parents if I was interested in going on a month-long road trip playing small towns across the province with a troupe of performers so varied as to include not just guitarists but puppeteers and modern dancers, the answer was obviously yes! And that's how I ended up spending two summers aboard a trashed old bus that often stank of weed, driving around to towns that were so small even I, a proud son of Saskatchewan, had never heard of some of them.

The project was called Communicart, and it was the brainchild of some of the leaders of our local arts scene, most notably Sandy Cameron, whose daughter, Kirsten, had been my kindergarten classmate. Sandy was a gifted fiddler and a major figure in Regina's creative circles, easily identified by his red, curly hair, which was always tucked into a tight ponytail. He was a gruff guy in some ways, seemed like he was all business, but he was always quick to laugh and was generally well-liked. Much of the project centred around a band he led, and I joined, called Sod Hut and the Buffalo Chips. I hated the name then, and still do today, but the music was exhilarating, swelling bluegrass-tinged jams with some Celtic and Métis energy in the mix too. But the tour was so much more than fiddlers, mandolin players, Irish pennywhistlers, and banjos. Elsewhere on the roster were singer-songwriters, performance artists, storytellers, and the beloved Little Red Hen children's theatre troupe.

One of the company's driving forces, and another of the big personalities in our group, was Ian Black, a tall, dark-haired actor/musician who would later appear occasionally on shows like Canada's iconic hit sitcom *Corner Gas*, among others. Ian was charismatic and handsome, and as silly as Sandy could be serious. He loved catchphrases and puns—"If I don't see you in the future, I'll see you in the pasture," or "It's not how high you are, it's hi how are you?" He'd often say things like this when we were on the road, which was sometimes funny because we were often camping in actual pastures and some of us were most likely high. Ian played guitar, too, and he'd seen the world, dropping acid on the top of the pyramids in Egypt, roaming the Middle East and exotic faraway cities like Beirut or Tangiers, and coming back with many tales to tell. He'd remain a friend and a big part of my life for many years, and I'll come back to him soon enough.

This roving gang of artists was funded by the Saskatchewan government, who'd given Sandy and the crew a small arts grant to support the program. The idea was that, by taking this ragtag cultural juggernaut to small towns throughout the province, we'd foster a strong sense of community and togetherness, and we'd encourage musicians and artists in the various places we visited to join in and perform with us—city folk meeting country folk in some kind of blissful artistic harmony of shared experience. Sometimes it worked, and we'd have big, loose jams and meet wonderful people. More often than not, it felt more like we were the circus freak hippies paraded in front of the head-scratching locals wondering if this was where their tax money was going. But either way, it didn't really matter to me. I was a kid, and these trips were heaven—a way to absorb everything I could from the older players around me like a musical sponge, absolutely, but also to absorb some important early lessons in how to get along with others in tight touring quarters.

I learned from everybody, but especially the Mahood brothers, David and Craig, who played the fiddle and mandolin respectively, and very well. I'd play with them off and on for years to come. Once, some years later, I was driving with one of the brothers to Saskatoon to play the Sundog Music Festival. At the time, I was deep into the pennywhistle, and we were driving down the highway while I whistled away, probably not very well. Craig Mahood was going through a recent breakup, a Communicart connection, actually; he'd just been unceremoniously dumped by Gloria, a core member of the Little Red Hen Story Theatre. Listening to an amateur practise the pennywhistle—which, incidentally, now costs about sixty dollars—in the enclosed space of a car is never a lot of fun, but especially if you're nursing a completely crushed heart. I kept mindlessly whistling my way north through the prairies, and at some point the quiet and usually reserved Craig Mahood just snapped. He reached across the car, grabbed the misery stick, and threw it straight out of the open passenger window, where it disappeared forever into the wheat fields. I guess silence soothes a broken heart a lot better than a poorly executed Celtic reel!

Because I was thirteen or fourteen, I didn't really drink alcohol while on our tours, but I do recall dabbling in weed a fair bit—rations of which were part of our modest compensation. Every day on the bus that summer, a big plastic garbage can of pre-rolled joints would get passed around, and each troupe member was allowed to take two.

We had some non-musical adventures too. There was the time we ran out of gas just outside one of our small-town destinations. Fortunately for us, we were on a slight downhill, and everyone on the bus started chanting, "Come on! Come on, you can make it!" as we rolled into the service station with mere seconds to spare. Or the time we played a place in northern Saskatchewan and the puppet show actors started to get heckled by the town drunk, who was then popped squarely in the jaw by an audience member right in front of all the locals and some of their kids. Nice.

We would stay anywhere we could when the caravan was touring, once camping on a hippie ranch that raised buffalo instead of cows. We went up north to Indigenous communities, where we were thought to be just as weird as we had been in the farm towns down south. There were countless long nights by the fire, playing mandolin and guitar and learning tunes until the sky started to lighten with the prairie dawn, the air filled with the most incredible birdsong.

We played one memorable show at a historic site called Batoche. This was the place where, in 1885, around nine hundred Canadian troops confronted and fought with the highly outmanned and outgunned Métis leader and spokesman Louis Riel and his tactical leader Gabriel Dumont and their three-hundred-man army. We set up our show as usual, making a little stage area close to the historic site, and waited for our audience to appear. As it got closer to showtime, we could see one vehicle slowly making its way down the valley towards us, way off in the distance. "Well, at least someone is showing up," we all thought as we stood there expectantly. The car finally came to a stop at the designated parking area, and we waited for the occupants to emerge. After a long moment a lone man in a wheelchair lowered himself mechanically to the ground and promptly wheeled himself over to watch the show. I'm not sure who started the show that night, but our sole audience member must not have liked what he saw or heard, because five minutes later he agonizingly repeated his entrance in reverse. It was a very short show that evening. Sadly hilarious.

I was unrecognizable to my parents upon my return, a scarf tied around my neck and a jauntily angled cap atop my head. What an amazing experience that summer had been. The memories included my first taste of beer in a bar, a stolen sip before the bartender realized I was underage and gave me the boot; and the first time I saw seriously dancing northern lights, sitting in a canoe, high as a kite with Kirsten and Suzy from our troupe, in the middle of a lake in one of the most beautiful places on earth.

All these experiences threaded together into two unforgettable trips, summers that transformed me. I set out on the road as a clean-cut, eager young kid, and I returned a hippie wanderer who had seen something of the world. I would never be the same again.

CHAPTER FOUR

AMERIPASS

"HOW ABOUT WE GO on a bus trip through the States, just me and you, on a Greyhound for two or three months?"

My mom was always full of surprises, but this was something new. In the late spring of 1977, I was in grade seven, and quite out of the blue she asked if I wanted to leave school a month early and hit the road. I think this would be a dream trip for most kids, or at least the ones who got along with their parents the way I did. The getting-out-of-school part would have appealed to anybody at that age—and especially to a kid who was struggling there, as I was. I was about to turn thirteen, in my last year of junior high, and my general loathing of all things school, especially the cliques, the jerks, and the school bullies, had already reached a full simmer. My hard musical work was starting to pay off. I was playing more and more guitar, and starting to make a name for myself around the folk music community as someone to watch, which made school even less attractive to me.

It was also the time of year—and everyone reading this who grew up on the Canadian prairies will know exactly what I'm talking about—when the Saskatchewan spring had reached its worst point: the flickering warmth of the sun having melted off the last of the snowbanks and the continual runoff turning the ground sticky with all the salt, snow, slush, dirt, cigarette butts, and dog shit that had been sealed in the ice for months. Who wouldn't want a break from that? So when my mom asked the question, I didn't hesitate. It didn't even strike me—or I guess anyone else for that matter—as odd that my mother would take time off work and pull me out of school for an epic Greyhound bus trip. She was not your conventional mom. She was a *cool* mom. The idea of the trip made sense, and she probably wanted to show me that she understood how much hell I was going through at school.

Over a two-month stretch, we would get on and off the Greyhound bus and go anywhere our funds and energy would take us. We travelled on what was called an Ameripass, which had been introduced in the early seventies, allowing unlimited travel within a ninety-nine-day window for a mere ninety-nine dollars. This was perfect for us, since my parents' social worker salaries, combined with a houseful of kids, meant we never had a lot of money. Our family believed that the essential nature of people was to be good and kind. After all, we were part of a larger spiritual community, and we were counting on our fellow Quakers throughout North America to see us through this upcoming road trip—a meandering itinerary of places to stay for free, or at least cheap.

Mom had written letters to everyone she knew or had a contact number for, one letter for every stop on our itinerary. She had a plan, and about a thousand dollars in traveller's cheques. I had a newspaper route, like most boys of my generation, but I knew I'd need more money than I had from that, so I threw all my Hardy Boys books into a big garbage bag and sold them to the kids on the school grounds at lunchtime and at recess. I can't be sure, but it's possible that a few of my sister's Nancy Drew books made it into that bag too—by accident, of course!

On May 29, 1977, my mom and I finally left Regina on a clear spring night, accompanied to the tired little Regina Greyhound bus station by my dad and my aunt Arlene. We then travelled through the night, with the dawn showing around Maple Creek, Saskatchewan, with its soft, rolling hills and antelope lying out in the fields, beautifully illuminated by the morning light. We continued on the southern route through Lethbridge, Alberta, where we caught the first sight of the mountains, like an illusion off in the distance. Breathtaking. We arrived in the little mountain town of Nelson, BC, where the movie *Roxanne*, staring Steve Martin, would be filmed exactly ten years later. We had crossed the Rockies into British Columbia, always a welcome change for me. In Nelson, my mom somehow found out that the Canada Post truck driver did a mail run up Kootenay Lake on Tuesdays and Thursdays, leaving early in the morning at 6 a.m. While she was trying to negotiate the next day's ride for us, standing just inside the Nelson post office, she realized in a panic that I had disappeared. She soon found me outside the door and around the corner, huddled on the curb, having just borrowed a street musician's guitar to strum a bit while I chatted with him amicably. This wouldn't be the last time I would pull a disappearing act.

We got up early to catch our Canada Post ride to the town of Kaslo—a one-hour trip that became more like a six-hour one since we had to keep stopping to deliver the mail. Once we arrived, we explored the town while the postman made his deliveries and then we all carried on driving around Kootenay Lake to the tiny community of Argenta, home of the Quaker Friends School. The town was mostly made up of Quakers, schoolteachers, 1960s draft dodgers, and various intellectuals from all over North America, an odd assortment of characters blissfully looking for a quieter way of life. We stayed with a lovely older woman named Betty Tillitson and her son Ben, who taught me to drive stick shift by tearing around their farm field in a cute little Volkswagen Bug.

Another family, the Sassamans, teachers at the local school, had us over for lunch. As we walked down the sloping gravel driveway to meet Bill and Donna, I was greeted, knocked down briefly, then humped by a giant Newfoundland cross named Herby. I learned later that his full name was Herbastion Von Shnoozer. I'd met the Sassaman family a few times before at springtime Quaker half-yearly meetings in Sorrento, when we would gather together in the beautiful mountain town resplendent in cherry and apple blossoms. I had become fast friends with their son Scott. He had two little sisters, the younger being Heather, who was five years younger than me. I remember vividly waiting for my turn at a buffet at one of those Sorrento meetings and sympathizing with her over the bad cold she'd come down with. Years later, after I was deep into my music career, we'd meet again, and that same Heather would become my wife and the mother of our two kids. But back then, she was just somebody's kid sister, and during our visit to her family's cabin on that road trip she was at her elementary school. Our paths wouldn't cross that day, but it's incredible to think that my future in-laws were standing right in front of me and I just didn't know it yet.

Once our northern circuit had been completed, Mom and I took the mail truck back to Nelson and got onto the Greyhound once again as we pushed farther west to the coast, to Vancouver, where the seventies west coast hippie culture was in full bloom. We stayed at the YMCA downtown, off Burrard Street, and rented bikes to ride around Stanley Park. We walked over the Burrard Street Bridge to the Vancouver Planetarium, a magical round theatre where you could settle back and watch the workings of the galaxy while Led Zeppelin's "Stairway to Heaven" and other mind-blowing tunes of the day like Pink Floyd's *Dark Side of the Moon* served as the soundtrack.

We saw all kinds of hippie kids strumming guitars and smoking pot on the local beaches, or just hanging out in front of Patti Fiedler's recently opened Soft Rock Café on 4th Avenue in Kitsilano, which was affectionately known as "the granola belt." One night we stayed with a friend of Mom's who was a Gestalt therapist, which, as far as the young me could tell, meant you sat inside a box and screamed until all the pain and anguish went away. My mom, who had trained as a psychiatric nurse, gave it a try. I'll say it again: My mom Joyce, who was forty-two years old at the time, was not a conventional mother. She was an older hipster who idolized the writer James Baldwin and believed passionately in racial equality and social justice, and she was game to try just about anything.

When we were ready to leave Vancouver, Mom and I made our way to the bus depot downtown, loaded our backpacks under the bus, and headed for the USA. First stop, Seattle.

It didn't take long to get into the rhythm of bus travel, which fostered a unique community of people united by the need to get somewhere the cheapest way possible. I laid claim to the seats behind the driver so I had a front-row view of the changing landscapes unfurling before me. Mom took the window seat and wrote endlessly in her diary. There were so many smells: the gag of diesel fumes from idling buses as we waited to board, the sun heating up the melting oil-stained asphalt in the station, and the always-present stench of urine and chlorine mixing together in the overused men's urinals of the station restroom and on the bus's privy. On the bus there was the unwelcome smell of humanity itself—fast food and endless cigarette smoke that hung in the air over our heads. In those days you could smoke almost anywhere—in university cafeterias, doctors' offices, planes, and also the back half of buses. In the dead quiet of night, when most of the passengers were asleep, I could even see the tiny red glow of the bus driver's cigarette moving in the dark between his face and the wheel. He'd open his window a crack and blow the smoke towards it.

As Mom slept, I watched the driver, and I watched the white line of the highway running out in front of the bus. My time on that bus journey would later inspire a song I wrote called "Far Away Like a Radio." The memories of that trip are gathered into a sort of collage of the mind, but they remain startlingly clear, as if, even then, I knew deep down that something pivotal was happening in my life. For a restless boy from the prairies, the trip opened the door to vast worlds I could never have imagined existed.

In Seattle, we stayed with my always irascible Serbian Grandpa Joe Buck and my sweet-natured Grandma Kay. They'd settled there after their years running the confectionary in Hope, BC. Joe worked as a machinist for Boeing, which had its headquarters in Seattle at the time. We stayed in their high-rise apartment in the suburbs, which was packed with cuckoo clocks that clamoured at all hours. When I was there, I got to eat exotic American cereal like Chex, the American version of Crispix, and I got to use the building's outdoor pool during our three-night stay.

One day at the crowded Pike Place Market I broke away from Grandma Kay and my mom. As I wandered, I befriended a gregarious Black busker who was playing some great-sounding blues on a National steel guitar, and I openly admired his cool blue military shirt with epaulettes on the shoulders, something I'd never really seen before but now found myself desperately wanting. The man sold it to me right then and there, quite literally the shirt off his back, for a few dollars. When I rejoined our party, I put it on without thinking twice, much to Grandma Kay's horror.

Mom went to a Baptist church on that visit, and she left me back at the apartment, where I happily swam in the pool. When she came back, she excitedly told me about the amazing gospel singing during the service and the heady soulfulness of it. I really regretted not experiencing this with her. I admired her bravery in simply walking into a church where she knew no one and then gleaning so much good from it.

Our next overnight stop was in San Francisco, where my mom had arranged to stay at the apartment of a man with connections to the Quakers back in Saskatchewan. We walked up three storeys and entered a filthy apartment, with dirty dishes piled high in the sink. In the spare room we slept under thin blankets on a flimsy mattress, stained like a map of the world. There were a few moments on our trip that filled me with some unease, and this stay was one of them. Not because it felt dangerous in any way, but because you could almost sense the loneliness and emptiness in the walls.

During the day, I took comfort in meandering along the famous fisherman's wharf with Mom, taking in the navy-blue San Francisco harbour where a twenty-eight-year-old Otis Redding had penned the posthumously released hit song "(Sittin' On) The Dock of the Bay."

The open sky and the sound of shrieking seagulls overhead, the pier filled with tourists, the famous Alcatraz prison off in the distance, and street musicians and jugglers plying their trade on the busy streets—it was all totally intoxicating. At the San Francisco wharf I'd stand, mouth agape, and watch these street buskers, so many of them talented and outgoing. I'd listen to them play, of course. But more than that, I'd watch them command an audience. I didn't know it, but I was soaking up the art of performance.

Los Angeles was a very different deal. The bus station was in an extremely seedy pocket of old downtown, close to the now-trendy Silver Lake area. It had a sign in the washroom that said DO NOT LEAVE YOUR CHILD UNATTENDED, which should give you a sense of the vibe. The bus stations we frequented were usually located in the roughest parts of town, and they were a hub for people who had nowhere else to go. There were people who wanted to sleep for a few hours on a hard plastic bench, or hide out in one of the washroom stalls, clanking around doing god knows what, or stay warm in the coffee shop, with fluorescent lights and dirty tabletops. The bus stations were congested swarms of random activity, not especially suitable or safe for a child, especially then, in the economically depressed urban centres of the 1970s. We didn't linger in LA, and instead got on another bus, heading for Phoenix.

In Phoenix, we had no Quakers to stay with, so Mom shelled out for one of only maybe three motels we would stay at on the whole trip. The room had a thin carpet and rough floral bedspreads. The small pool out front was the saving grace, and I needed it; the desert sun beat down hard, and the heat was so intense, it felt like the life was being sucked out of me. We only stayed one night, mercifully, and we kept moving deeper into America. As we went, it all became more foreign to me, more potentially fraught, but thus more exciting too. The accents became thicker, and the bus filled with more traditionally religious people, as well as lots of regular folks who couldn't afford another means of transport—just like us! At night, the back of the bus would often become a party zone, voices growing louder as strangers got into the hooch and became quick friends. Technically, booze wasn't allowed on board, but a bus driver could only do so much to keep the peace in such an environment. When we couldn't secure our favourite seats up front, Mom and I would be forced to look for space closer to the back, where sometimes I would overhear conversations that were not, let's say, meant for ears as young as mine.

Next we stopped in Flagstaff and stayed with a kind, elderly Quaker lady who was into astronomy and had a prosthetic arm. I was not a shy kid, and I asked if she'd let me touch her mechanical fingers, which she graciously allowed. Flagstaff had a famous observatory that you could see right from the window of the nice Quaker woman's place. At the Grand Canyon we stopped for a visit and, as usual, I wandered off. I hiked into the canyon, along a narrow, circuitous path, and got chatting on the way with a girl my age. We kept heading down the path hoping to reach Indian Plateau, a cool spot that gave you an awesome view of the bottom of the canyon. The distance was deceiving and eventually we realized we were not going to make it that far, so we turned around to head back up. We had no water with us and were gone for three or four hours. By the time I got back to the top, my mother was frantic, although I also suspected she'd made some friends and had mostly been enjoying herself at the trailhead restaurant where she had met some fellow travellers, until she realized how long I'd been gone.

In Wichita, Kansas, we stayed at a university dormitory and Mom attended a big conference with Quakers from all over the world. She participated in various sessions where everyone would sit in a circle and take turns talking, probably sharing things about their personal spiritual path or other Quaker issues of the day. Bored out of my mind, I found an outdoor basketball game with some kids. We were there a few days, and I'm sure Mom was relieved to be around like-minded people her own age for a while. I made fast friends and wandered around the large campus goofing off and drinking my new favourite soft drink, Dr Pepper. We were told by others at the conference that we might find that Quakers could get slightly more religious the farther east and south we went, and to keep that in mind when we were looking for a place to stay going forward.

We made our way through Texas and Arkansas, and finally got to New Orleans late one night, where the summer humidity was suffocating and swelling, at least as far as Mom's ankles went. Outside the bus station, a kindly African American man stopped us and said, "Ma'am, you shouldn't be out here with your son in this neighbourhood at this time of night." Being from Saskatchewan, we may have been naive, but we never really felt afraid. Perhaps we should have been. We decided to find our pre-arranged lodging in the morning and spent the night inside the bus station. In these situations I would invariably bug my mom for quarters to plug into the little automatic televisions that were attached to the hard plastic seats so I could watch *The Mary Tyler Moore Show* or an episode of *M*A*S*H*.

When morning broke, we walked for a bit and then boarded a streetcar trolley that looked straight out of an old black-and-white movie. We eventually arrived at the house where we were to billet. After a light knock on the door, a testy middle-aged woman cautiously opened the heavy wooden slab, and that's when I saw that there were only two holes in the middle of her face where her nose should have been. I stared in horror while my mom stammered, "We're the Quakers from Canada who phoned a while back about staying here for a night." Between this woman and the armless lady in Flagstaff, I started to wonder why a lot of Quakers were missing body parts. The woman in New Orleans wasn't pleased, not pleased at all, and said something about this not being a hotel and that we were a day late. Grudgingly, she opened the door and let us in.

We were tired, Mom especially, but I badgered her for us to get out and explore the city. I remember the green, pink, and yellow Creole houses, the front porches, the fragrant gardenia flowers, and the world-famous Café du Monde, where I begged my mom for their powdered beignets. But best of all, and the thing I'd looked forward to most, were the street musicians playing blues, jazz, and second line. We even crammed inside the historic Preservation Hall and caught the famous house ragtime band in the sepia-toned little building that looked like a movie set. As we walked through the French Quarter, my head swam with the humidity, the endless music, the lineups of people, the nearly choking aromas of fried foods and cigar smoke, and the way people enunciated their words, all so foreign to my Saskatchewan ears. But the heat was an oppressive weight that wouldn't let up, and Mom desperately wanted to get back to our room. We had our first big fight because I wanted to stay at Louis Armstrong Park and linger over the statues and watch the jazz bands, and not go back to the house with the noseless lady who didn't even want us there.

The trip was tiring us out and we started to bicker more frequently, struggling with rising temperatures and hosts who were becoming equally inhospitable. In Mobile, Alabama, we found respite visiting with Mom's old acquaintance Dr. Osmond, the doctor who had experimented in psychedelics back at Weyburn Hospital. There, I ate my first kumquat and secretly fell in love with his beautiful, strawberry blond–haired daughter, who was just slightly older than me. Later, at the motel in Mobile, I went swimming in the pool while my mom was hassled by a tacky businessman who was obviously trying to put the moves on her. "Get out of here, creep!" I thought to myself.

Mom made sure I got to see Walt Disney World in Orlando, which delighted me. But in "The Happiest Place on Earth" we also fought more, dragging ourselves over broiling asphalt streets and through miserable lineups. Sometimes when we argued, I'd storm off, but never go far enough to lose sight of her.

After a long day wandering in beautiful but sleepy St. Petersburg, I remember peering around corners after another heat-induced argument to ensure she was visible at a distance. Mom was careful not to lose sight of me, either, no matter how irritated she was with me. We ended up laughing later at the absurdity of it all, trying to stay angry as we struggled to keep each other in our sightlines.

Back on the bus, we continued our journey, ending up at a place called the Friends Society in Tallahassee, Florida. Mom had chosen it because "Friends Society" sounded a lot like the typical Quaker house's name, the Society of Friends. An unshaven man opened the door and showed us to our sparse room on the second floor. We were so exhausted when we arrived that we threw our bags down and flaked out on the bed, but soon realized that the window had a large hole in the middle of it with jagged broken glass all around the edges. Gaunt, jittery men kept walking in and out of adjacent rooms, and it became clear this was no Quaker house or hostel, but rather a halfway house for addicts of all kinds. Mom and I were both nervous, but we were also so tired. We fell asleep instantly, only to be awakened at four in the morning when a man walked straight into our room. My mother called out in a sleepy stupor and the would-be murderer left instantly. We crept out of the nightmare house at the break of dawn, relieved to have survived. On the bus, we slept like babies.

We were now heading towards North Carolina, where we would be staying with a young Quaker family that lived in a wooded rural area and also had a super-cool zip line to play on and kids my age to hang out with. From there we made our way to the famous country music mecca of Nashville, Tennessee, where we went to the Grand Ole Opry and visited Ernest Tubb's record store. Mom said: "Okay, I have twenty-five dollars left, that's it. Do we buy records or save it for food?" Naturally, we chose the records, and I remember we picked up some Hank Williams and a Louvin Brothers album.

In my mind, Nashville was the trip's last major destination—the rest were just stops on the way home. Somewhere between Minnesota and North Dakota, Mom turned to me and abruptly asked, "How would you feel if your dad and I split up?" The question hung in the air like a heavy black cloud. After a prolonged, interminable silence, thick and suffocating, I stammered the only thing I could think to say—"Not very good!"

We sat in complete stillness, staring at the road ahead. After some time, she went back to scribbling in her journal, the relentless writing being her way of filling the silence. I shifted in my seat, realizing that this trip hadn't been just about a mother-and-son adventure after all. It actually all revolved around this very question. Later, we crossed into Canada, exhausted and starving, and headed to our friends' place, the Ackermans', in Winnipeg, where we ate heartily and slept soundly. The next day we travelled back home to Regina, where my dad met us at the station and carried our bags to the familiar green International Harvester. Life went on normally for a while, until one day it didn't. My parents were splitting up, and life would never be the same.

Later that summer, after the epic bus trip, my dad wanted to take me camping in the Rockies. We both loved the mountains, and I think he wanted to have his own adventure with me, something to match the one I'd had with Mom. So Dad, my brother Murray, and I packed up the old Travelall with our aged camping gear and headed west.

Our destination was near Banff, a place we'd been a few years earlier for a Quaker gathering called Peak Experience. We'd loved the hiking there, and I was excited to return. The campsite itself was on what's known as the 1A, a scenic highway that runs between Banff and Lake Louise; it was the old road people used before the more modern and wider one was put in, and it was the perfect place for those looking to camp a bit off the beaten path. We stopped at a place called Johnson's Canyon, which boasted a short hiking trail up to a spectacular waterfall. We'd done the little hike when we were told that the trail actually continued for quite a while beyond the falls, higher into the backcountry, where we could camp. We began hauling our gear up, the first load anyway, heading into the unknown to find our campsite.

We climbed past the falls again and made our way up a marked path for a few kilometres, until we found a good, open place to pitch our oversized canvas tent. I'd started feeling a bit sick on the walk due to the altitude. I was unsteady, my head pounding, so I helped to set up camp until I couldn't help anymore. Then I sat there with my face in my hands, eyes closed, which seemed to bring a bit of relief. Dad and Murray went back to the car for the rest of the stuff while I writhed about, feeling terrible. Sometime that evening a park ranger came by and informed us that there was a grizzly bear active in the area, so we had to be sure to put everything away and hang our food up in a tree. This naturally set my anxiety off. Between my worried, sick moaning and the spectre of a killer predator, I barely slept. At first light we started packing up, and we made a plan: We'd carry what we could down, delivering me to safety (and a lower altitude), and I'd hang out in the parking lot of the local motel while Dad and Murray made another trip to bring down the rest of our gear.

As luck would have it, the owners of the motel had a daughter about my age, and as my altitude sickness abated, she and I became fast friends, roaming all over the property as she showed me around. By the time Murray and Dad got back, hours later, I was in the motel diner, enjoying a milkshake with my new friend, feeling slightly guilty for not feeling worse physically. They were beat from all the hiking, and it was too late to try and find a spot to camp elsewhere, so we decided to stay put and sleep in the Travelall that night—illegal, technically, since it was in a national park, but we were all too tired and rattled to care.

Late that evening, around 9 p.m., I had the thought that it would be nice to get a postcard from the gift shop to send to Mom back home. I approached the motel doors and noticed that they were slightly ajar in an unusual way. As I pushed them open, I called out a hello, which was greeted by a strange rustling coming from the room behind the front desk. A man emerged with a garbage bag in his hand and some sort of mask on his head. For a second I froze, realizing I had just interrupted a robbery. Then I turned around and ran, careful to close the door fully behind me.

As I beat it across the parking lot, I was certain I was done for. Any second I'd feel the wallop of a bullet entering my back, or I'd be grabbed by the rough hands of a robber, or maybe even the long arm of the law, who might mistake me for an accomplice. Wrong place, wrong time, I thought, and this would be the end of me. But miraculously, I made it back to the car, and I regaled Murray and Dad with the story. They acted concerned, but I got the distinct feeling they in no way bought my story. But sweet vindication came in the form of a police officer knocking on the window of our car at five the next morning. First, he expressed his dismay at our illegal parking. And second, he wanted to know if we'd seen anything suspicious the night before, because they were investigating an incident at the motel.

I probably said I told you so all the way back to Saskatchewan.

CHAPTER FIVE

END OVER END

FROM MY BEDROOM WINDOW looking down on 24th Street, I watched quietly as my world changed forever. It was a fall day in 1977, leaves on the ground and barren branches swaying in the wind. On the prairies, summer sometimes lingers, mixing with autumn, with the weather moving back and forth between the two seasons. And sometimes autumn arrives in full force, stripping the trees, chilling the air, greying the skies, and darkening the mood, or at least mine. From the perch where just years before I'd launched paper airplanes, dreaming of flying away, I watched someone else take flight—my mother, Joyce. I don't remember the date, but it must have been a weekend, because I was home instead of being in school. But my dad wasn't there—he was conspicuously absent, and fair enough. Mom was moving out, and doing so with the help of her new boyfriend, Herb Strongeagle, a man I'd not yet met even as I watched him load box after box of my mom's possessions into the back of his pickup truck parked out front.

My mom's question on the bus months before had been a warning. Things between her and my dad had apparently got pretty bad, worse than I knew. I had inklings—there had been the time I found Mom crying by herself on the couch, and in the weeks after we returned from our Ameripass trip I could sometimes hear the intense murmurs of my parents arguing in the next room when I lay in bed. But this day still came as a shock. I can't remember who broke the news to me, but it finally came out that Mom had begun a new relationship with a man named Herb, and that she would be leaving to live with him. As I watched them carrying her stuff out to the car, returning to the house, then doing it again and again, I realized they had been together for a while. You could see it in the small gestures, the way they cared for each other, the way they communicated with tilts of the head, soft touches on the arm. They were familiar, which made it all the worse; this wasn't some crazy fling that would end soon. I couldn't have known it then, but my mom and Herb Strongeagle would be together for the rest of her days. It would be his hand I held as I watched my mother leave this world nearly fifty years later.

Herb had been married before, I'd come to learn, but his young wife had been tragically killed in a random shooting in a bar downtown, leaving Herb with a four-year-old son, a very cute kid named Brad. My mom would move in with them, and help raise Brad.

At our house on 24th Street, it was just me and my dad at this point, my siblings having scattered to BC, and the place felt cavernous and empty once Mom left. In the months that followed, my dad and I tried to settle into new routines. I kept cleaning the house and Dad tried to cook the meals and help me with my homework. But he always had this look on his face of someone in shock, walking away from a terrible car accident. When I got a little older, I'd come to see that my father had a problem with depression, and probably always had. But we never spoke about it. One day he came home with a new car, a bright-yellow Dodge Maverick, a sporty little two-door thing with a dual racing stripe stretching up the hood. Looking back, it feels very on-brand for a mid-life-crisis moment, but I don't really remember what I thought of it at that point. I'd give anything to be able to hear what the two of us said when I first walked out and saw that thing in the driveway!

We must have made quite a pair, actually, sad Bill Munn and his anxious teenage son. I felt bad for my dad, and worried about how he would cope with it all—how *we* would cope with it all. And I wasn't alone. All around town we'd get concerned looks from people filled with pity that drove me crazy. I remember going to a brand new trendy coffee shop, a place that would turn out to have killer carrot cake, where old family friends looked at me with sympathy. "How are you and your father doing?" they'd ask. I hated that. In response, I decided I would act as though nothing out of the ordinary was happening, nothing at all, and I'd deflect their concerns, hardening myself from then on. "We're fine," I'd snap back, my armour becoming stronger with each reply.

But that first day, as I watched the empty pickup truck bed fill with what felt like my childhood itself, I wasn't so hardened yet. If I'm being honest, I was heartbroken. Herb and my mom pulled away from the curb, taking with them the life I'd known, and I sat on the bed and cried. Then, as I would do for the rest of my life, I started to work through it the best way I knew how. I picked up my guitar.

My mom and Herb moved into a rented Craftsman-style house near 13th Avenue, and for reasons I was never totally clear on, Mom left social work and took a job as a waitress in a diner on the corner of Albert and 13th, not far from their house. Sometimes I'd meet her there for lunch, harkening back to our old Woolworth lunch counter days, but it was different now. It was odd to see her working in a place like that, and I'm embarrassed to say it now, but back then I didn't like it. It was a time of confronting prejudices within myself, work that extended to my feelings about her dating an Indigenous man. I'd grown up in a progressive household and been quick to educate my classmates on the plight of Indigenous peoples in Canada whenever I overheard a negative comment or stereotype. But now I came face to face with the fact that, as open-minded as I believed myself to be, I felt uneasy about my mom's new love. I was deeply embarrassed by those feelings, but I would come to realize that acknowledging that such things exist even within oneself is an important part of not just understanding the way racism functions in our world but starting to move past it.

Herb was from the Pasqua reserve near Regina, and he had a master's degree in finance from the University of Ottawa. At the time, he worked as a financial manager for a few of the bands near us in Saskatchewan and beyond. Later, I would learn that he was a survivor of the horrific and genocidal residential school system, but at the time I was probably more interested in his notoriety as a famous local hockey player. I wasn't ready to like him yet—I had so much anger about what was happening to our family—but I was sure impressed by him.

I rarely, if ever, set foot in the house he shared with my mother on 13th Street, because not long after Mom moved out, she and Herb moved away to Whitehorse. Mom arranged for me to come visit during spring break when I was fourteen years old. It's a long way from Regina to the Yukon, and I'll never forget the exhilaration of looking out that airplane window and seeing the prairies give way to what seemed like endless ranges of jagged mountains erupting up out of the flat plains. As I settled in, I struck up a conversation with an older woman sitting beside me. I excitedly told her all about my trip, about Mom and Herb, about how eager I was to see Whitehorse. Neither she nor I could possibly have known that I'd end up spending much of my life in the air. And she was nice to me, even though nobody wants to be seated next to the hyper kid flying for the first time. At some point, the flight attendant came around with food, and I could not believe my good fortune—a cloth napkin held real silverware. I had my own little salt and pepper shakers, and in the middle of the tray, a beautiful steak. (Air travel has changed a bit over the decades!) As I started to cut my steak, my knife slipped and the entire filet popped right off my plate into my neighbour's lap. I was mortified and full of apologies, but she just laughed it off and we continued on our way. So much for repaying a kindness!

Mom, Herb, and little Brad were living in a complex of identical townhouses on the outskirts of Whitehorse, which is where we headed after they picked me up at the airport. I arrived after dark, and I remember feeling so excited to be this far north. The next day, I couldn't wait to see the town in the light, when Mom drove me around, showing off her new surroundings. We visited the antique paddle steamer called the SS *Klondike*, which had been launched in 1929 (the same year my dad was born), and which was now a tourism magnet, dry docked next to the Yukon River. We wandered around downtown, which held a smattering of stores selling outdoor gear and some gold rush–themed hotels and funky little coffee shops. We took a drive south to a small town called Carcross, near the BC border, where we stopped for pie and coffee at the Caribou Hotel, home of the famous parrot Polly, who had died just a few years earlier at the ripe old age of 126. Polly apparently sang, swore, drank liquor, and greeted guests with his favourite song, "I Love You Truly." By the time we turned up, he'd been succeeded by two more talking parrots. Unlike Polly, they wouldn't live their lives among miners and prospectors, so I don't know if they ever learned to swear quite as robustly.

On that trip I also got to know Herb a little bit better, and I found him to be a friendly and fun person, full of *joie de vivre*—naturally gregarious and adventurous, just like my mom. Years later, back in Saskatchewan, he would be the first person to show me the cover of Stevie Ray Vaughan's debut album, *Texas Flood*. The cover bears a painting of Stevie dressed in a Mexican-style serape holding a black Stratocaster. I believe Herb thought he was purchasing an album by a Cherokee or Apache southwestern blues player—fair enough, given Stevie's garb—and he was excited to share it with me. Not long after that, Stevie would show up in *People* magazine and on David Bowie's iconic song "Let's Dance" and change the worlds of both young Colin Munn and blues guitar itself forever.

Whitehorse was a place where a lot of people moved to get away from city life, and it was fascinating for me to explore this beautiful place full of loners, rounders, nature lovers, and draft dodgers, all caught up in the magnetic pull of the north. And Mom and Herb worked hard to make me feel welcome, going so far as to book me a guest slot with a local band called Whiskey Jack at their gig at the nearby Kopper King bar. Whiskey Jack played a blend of folk, rock, and Celtic music, and while I was right at home musically, I was underage, so I had to wait behind the kitchen doors in the staff lounge for my turn to play. When they finally called me out, I had a ball, and it was a really cool thing to be able to play mandolin in front of my mom and Herb in their new hometown.

Aside from jamming at the Kopper King, my clearest memory from that visit was actually something I saw on TV. April 7, 1979,

Saturday night in Whitehorse, all of us gathered around the television to watch the still relatively new show *Saturday Night Live*, where musical guest Rickie Lee Jones was about to blow our collective socks off. Rickie Lee stepped up to the mic with a pink tam set at a jaunty angle and rasped out the opening lines of her new hit song, "Chuck E.'s in Love." I was as smitten by the music as I was by her funky stage presence—rock music with a groovy, syncopated beat, sung with style and grace and a unique sensibility. The year before, Mark Knopfler and Dire Straits had released their first full-length masterpiece, and everything was starting to shift for me. My Celtic and traditional period was waning as the broader musical currents changed. The world had started to be transformed by punk and new wave, and all of us were going to go along for the musical ride in one way or another. I could feel it all mixing inside me, and I was ready for what was next, what was new.

On my return flight to Regina, the plane had a layover in Edmonton. I fell asleep in a hard little plastic seat only to awaken and discover I'd missed my connection. These were the days before apps and reminders, and I panicked. I tearfully pleaded with the woman at the desk to help me find my way home. I can't quite remember how it all played out, but I got back to Saskatchewan eventually. And when I did, a new era began.

My first semester of grade nine at Sheldon Williams High School went well enough, especially given the reputation that the Munn kids and our Konrad cousins had in those halls. I'd heard horror stories about Mr. Boychuck, the extremely strict principal with whom my brother Robbie had somehow ended up in a fist fight. Robbie had long hair, and in those days that was enough to get you on the wrong side of the administration. As if that wasn't enough, Robbie had been nearly expelled after he and my cousin Kenny threw a pack of lit firecrackers into Vice-Principal Philpot's office. Despite this disorderly legacy, I got off to a fine enough start, but by second semester things started to change. By then I'd joined a new band, playing songs by the Police, the Cars, Television, the Clash, and other punk and new wave bands that were leading the musical charge at the time. I'd been introduced to that music by a local tastemaker named Mike Burns, who loved the Jam and Bryan Ferry and who pretty much singlehandedly dragged Regina into the punk era. Mike wasn't a musician himself, but he had a strong sensibility and shaped countless local minds with his great aesthetics. Mike's encouragement had been the final push I needed to start to sever ties with my folk world and plunge headfirst into a new musical direction.

I also plunged headfirst into smoking cigarettes, weed, and hash, and I started skipping school. I'd still play with my folk friends from time to time, but now I felt slightly embarrassed by them and the music we'd all play together. It didn't feel cool enough, and I wanted to distance myself from all that, though it proved tricky after a guy named Ted Turner, a high-up in the local bike gang the Apollos, heard I had started smoking and turned my back on the folkies. He threatened to break my fingers if he saw me smoking, just to give me a scare. Ted had a tough exterior, but he had a soft side too, and he loved playing the dulcimer, of all things. His had a beautiful dragon's head with ivory teeth inlaid into the middle of the headstock. He was just sticking up for his tradition, I guess.

The band I was playing with at that time had a few different names, and for a while we settled on Nick Danger and the Close Calls. We'd play house parties and private gatherings and the occasional gig at a city festival or celebration. We started getting a little coverage in the local press, and we began opening for the Extroverts, the most popular punk/new wave band in the area. We were a lot younger than those guys, and they loved teasing us. For one show, when we were once again uncertain of what to call ourselves, the Extroverts advertised us on the posters and introduced us to the crowd as the Wankers. We were mortified, and pissed that they'd taken such liberties, but we kind of said what the hell—at least we were playing shows. We rolled our eyes, but we rolled with the name too. From then on we were the Wankers.

That second semester of grade nine, as all things scholastic started going quickly downhill for me, a wonderful, caring teacher named Mrs. McCalpine took me aside and asked me why I would sit by myself and not participate in band class. I was failing, and she couldn't understand why. I explained that it was nothing personal, I just wanted to be by myself for the period and play my guitar and mandolin, treating it like a break from math, science, and all the other school stuff I hated. She was nice about it, but I knew she couldn't help me if I wouldn't take part. For reasons I can't quite recall, I did agree to one act of participation: playing the lead guitar solo with the school band on the Commodores song "Easy" at the end-of-year school concert. For the show, I borrowed a friend's dad's white Strat, and in true rock star fashion I dropped a hit of acid to help enhance my big moment. Apparently, I had soloed for around five minutes before someone finally caught my attention, frantically giving me the universally understood "wrap it up" gesture. I still failed ninth grade music class.

My efforts to spend more time with people my own age were aided greatly by a new friendship with a charismatic kid from school named Nathan Wiens, who, along with Colin Linden, was one of the few people I met at that time who remains a lifelong friend. Nathan came from a family that seemed slightly more refined and somehow elite to me at the time; he had not just a pool table but an *actual* pool. The Wiens family lived on Albert Street, where Regina's well-to-do resided, in a huge house in which each room had a different-coloured ceiling. Nathan's family was artsy, maybe a classier version of the hippie scene I'd come up with. His dad was an architect in the modern, concrete minimalist style, and his sister, Robin, had been one of my babysitters. Nathan had five sisters, actually, and they all looked like Swedish models, blond and beautiful. Those sisters had turned Nathan on to lots of great records—Patti Smith, Nina Simone, Roxy Music—and Nathan and I hit it off right away. He was a good-looking kid with high cheekbones and messy hair, often found riding a skateboard, and we started hanging out and partying together. We had a little crew, and we walked the streets at night like a bunch of hoodlums. These kids were mostly the children of people wealthier than my parents, and with that, I noticed, came a certain entitlement. To my horror, they'd snap antennas off random cars or raid people's immaculately tended vegetable gardens. I didn't want to stand out, so I'm embarrassed to say I didn't do anything to stop this, and just let it happen around me.

Nathan and I started wearing safety pins in our ripped T-shirts and jackets and listening to "God Save the Queen" by the Sex Pistols, while getting kicked out of art class for our bad attitudes. Hanging out with Nathan always felt semi-dangerous in an exhilarating way. You never knew where you would end up. One minute you were going for lunch at a friend's house and the next minute the hot knives were out to smoke some hash before heading back to class. One night we crashed at Nathan's place after drinking and carousing till the wee hours, and I'll never forget waking up on the floor of their billiards room in a semi-drunken state as we were soundly admonished by Mrs. Wiens. "It smells like a liquor store in here!"

One day in the summer after grade nine, Nathan asked if I'd like to go to a party out in Fort Qu'Appelle. Somebody's parents owned a cottage, and it was going to be epic. We went with our usual gang, and we showed up at the property in the late afternoon. It was a crazy scene on a lake with people swimming and water-skiing, maybe a few hundred kids gathered there. I knew a lot of them, and it was a good time for a while. When it started getting late, I tried to find

Nathan so that we could head back to Regina. But I couldn't find him anywhere—he'd disappeared. A good Quaker boy at heart, I just wanted to go home. I started getting anxious, and then I started panicking. How was I going to get back? I ended up accepting a ride with a guy I really didn't like who loaded up his car with my fellow drunk teens. We tore off down a dirt road, and quickly I started asking the driver to take it easy. Everybody else was passed out, nobody was wearing a seat belt, and I didn't even notice us start to drift off the road because I was too busy leaning over into the front seat begging the guy to slow down.

The wheels of the car caught the loose shoulder before it flipped end over end two or three times, ending up upside down in a field. The back window was broken, people were crying. It was terrifying, and some of my fellow passengers were seriously injured. And what did the driver do? What was his very first action, before he checked on a single person? He went and hid his beer in the field so the police who he knew would be coming wouldn't find it. My friend Terry was thrown from the car, and she and another friend, Andrew, both ended up in traction for months. I went to the hospital, where a doctor carefully removed the glass embedded all down my lower back. In the end, I was lucky. But it was a wake-up call. This new scene was potentially dark and dangerous. And it was time to think about making some changes.

My academic slide continued, and things were rough at home. My dad and I were fighting a lot, and he had to work harder and harder to get me out of bed after late nights spent with the Wankers or partying with my friends. I was sullen and grumpy in the mornings and probably hell to live with. I was skipping class even more, and doing terribly in school when I bothered to show up. One day, the intercom system crackled to life and the entire school was treated to the ominous voice of Mr. Boychuck summoning me: "Could student Colin Munn please report to the principal's office?" I made my way, knowing no good would be coming of this invitation.

"Sit down," Mr. Boychuck barked when I appeared in his doorway.

I took my seat and braced myself.

"It's come to my attention that your already terrible marks have taken a turn for the worse this year, Mr. Munn. Let me see here," he said as he consulted some papers, shuffling them around on his desk. "Ah yes, here it is. It seems that you have opted to attend only your English, art, and music classes, and have completely dropped out of science and all other academics."

I didn't know what to say, so I didn't say anything. He didn't seem to mind—he was going to do the talking. He looked at me sternly over the top of his horn-rimmed glasses.

"You will never graduate high school like this, Mr. Munn. In fact, given these efforts, you might as well quit."

He meant to scold me, scare me straight, but I heard another very profound truth. Mr. Boychuck was absolutely right! What *was* I doing here? Going through the motions for no particular reason, wasting precious time? I knew what I wanted—a life in music. And sitting around failing tenth grade English class and hanging out with my new friends who were my own age wasn't going to get me any closer to that. I looked out his window and saw the blue sky of possibility.

"Mr. Munn?" Mr. Boychuck said. "Am I boring you?"

"No, sir," I said. "You're not boring me at all. I was just sitting here realizing that you're right."

"Very good," he said. "Does that mean we can expect you to apply yourself going forward?"

"Oh, no. I didn't mean you were right about that. I meant you're right that I might as well quit! I'll never pass like this anyway. It's great advice. Thank you, sir. This really has been most helpful."

I can't remember if Mr. Boychuck said anything as I walked out the door of his office into my new life.

CHAPTER SIX

WINNIPEG-BOUND

BY 1980, THE WINNIPEG Folk Festival, which had been founded a mere six years earlier, had become a huge success. My family and I had gone a number of times during that period. But this summer was different. I wasn't there with my family or with a roving band of musical misfits I was touring with. No, this time I was enjoying the festival with friends from Regina, basically on my own for the first time, camping on the grounds. Also there were the Ackermans, our Quaker friends from Winnipeg, and more specifically their daughter Sunshine, whom I started to develop quite the crush on during that year's festival. To this day, the festival takes place on the same site it did then, north of downtown. A huge open field hosts the main stage, and the groves of beautiful old trees all around it house smaller stages. Paths snake through these trees, each of them taking you to some different destination where you might hear the next big thing.

But the main stage is always the main stage, the showcase for the headliners, and that year it featured none other than the legendary blues harmonica player and singer James Cotton. While most of my energy on that trip was spent trying to charm Sunny Ackerman, when Cotton took the stage, everything else fell away. He was electric, and his band was unbelievably tight. As his hard-charging music echoed around the trees, I realized I'd never heard anything quite like it—soulful, funky, bluesy, and just totally riveting. I think that was the moment, more than any other, that cemented the path I'd ultimately take in my life. I stood there in that field and realized that was it, *that* was what I wanted to do: play the blues live in front of thousands of people, making for them the same magic Cotton had made for me. Some years later I'd be up on that main stage myself, but I had a tougher go of it than Cotton did that night—I was playing some new music, and my lyric sheets kept blowing away in the prairie wind. But even then I did not lose sight of just how magical that spot was. It changed me forever.

Everything else in my life was changing too, and the pull of young love and Winnipeg's broader horizons was intense. That fall, after returning home to Regina, I couldn't get out of town fast enough; any chance I got, I'd be on the eight-hour Greyhound ride to Winnipeg to see Sunny. It was on one of those trips, returning to Regina on

December 8, that I heard the terrible news that John Lennon had been shot and killed in New York City. The driver got on the intercom and announced this sad fact to a busload of passengers. We all sat there, shocked and kind of numb for the rest of the ride. It was a feeling I had a lot at the time—kind of numb. That whole fall it was like I was performing a charade of being rooted in Regina. As soon as I could, I'd be back on the bus. The one thing I did with enthusiasm was continue to perform in our little rock band, the Wankers. Soon enough we were playing more and more shows, sometimes opening for pretty big names in the nascent Canadian punk rock and new wave scene passing through, bands like D.O.A., Teenage Head, and the Subhumans.

Once, we opened for the talented Art Bergmann, lead singer of the punk stalwarts the Young Canadians, at the Regina student union. Art would later play with Los Popularos, and John Cale of the Velvet Underground would produce his first solo record. But that night, I have the clearest memory of him throwing his vintage Strat, covered in stickers, way up in the air during a song, barely catching it as it came back down. Effortlessly cool! He invited me backstage after that show, and he was so encouraging and inclusive. We'd meet again a few years later in Vancouver and become friends, and later on we'd get together at my place in Lions Bay to attempt writing a song together. But at that time, he was just someone in a real touring band to look up to.

Later that December, after the John Lennon bus ride, I received a phone call from the Ackermans, asking if I'd be interested in accompanying Sunshine, her older sister Rain, her younger brother Stephen, her mom Caroline, and Caroline's beau, Tom Findley, on a road trip, heading from Winnipeg, travelling all the way through Colorado, New Mexico, and then on to Florida, where we'd spend Christmas at a beach house of a friend of Caroline's in St. Augustine before returning to Winnipeg after New Year's. I couldn't believe my good fortune—another American road trip, just a few years after my Ameripass adventure with my mom. A ticket out of Regina and a chance to spend the holiday in the Florida warmth within the proximity of Sunny, my new crush. It was a jackpot, and I couldn't say yes fast enough. All I had to do was convince my dad—but in the end he required no convincing. He'd seen us together that summer when Sunny visited me in Regina, and so he understood there was more than a childhood friendship going on here.

I felt bad leaving Dad alone for the holidays while I went off to pursue a new life of adventure. But when the day came to depart, I said my goodbyes and got back on the bus. Another eight hours, but on the other side, a kind of paradise.

We began our journey south by crossing from Manitoba into North Dakota, where the weather was bad and the roads were worse. I finally had my driver's licence, so I could at least help spell off Caroline and Tom on the drive. I remember plowing through the winter dark, everyone else in our little Datsun sound asleep. The wind picked up and the snow was blowing, totally blocking my view sometimes.

Beneath the snow you could feel the dangerous wobble of black ice. I was going as slow as I safely could, but that meant being passed by the huge semi-trailers. Every time one went past, the car windshield would get totally covered by freezing slush kicked up by the huge tires, and I'd be totally blinded for ten seconds or so. At one point I had to stop the car in the middle of the road and get out to see if I could find the painted lines I was meant to be driving between. Some scary stuff.

By the time we got to Colorado, the conditions had improved, and the drive towards our first destination, Taos, New Mexico, was truly stunning. I was used to beautiful Western landscapes, but this was something special. In Taos, we dropped young Stephen off at a clown camp that was being run at a little community called the Lama Foundation, situated fairly high on the side of a mountain in a series of semi-open-air buildings. It was, and as far as I know still is, a multi-faith-based meditation and retreat centre. Sunny's mother Caroline, although a Quaker, was a "seeker" and also studied Sufism and the teachings of Gurdjieff. The rest of us checked out views from the tops of cool geothermal-heated buildings, many of which were completely windowless and had outdoor showers with pull strings. I was smoking by this time, but smoking was strictly forbidden in the community, which meant I was constantly sneaking around looking for places to puff and then hide my cigarette butts. It was hard to be a fledging punk rocker at a spiritual retreat.

I fell in love with New Mexico and the dry desert topography, vast expanses with mountains looming at the edges. Sunny and I spent our lone night there sleeping on the floor of the main community centre, where we woke in the late morning to all kinds of people moving around our little mattress and sleeping bag, busy getting things ready for the kids' daycare the building also housed. I stumbled into some sort of shared kitchen and took a jar of yogurt out of the fridge for our breakfast. Somehow, it slipped from my hands and shattered on the floor, sending yogurt and shards of glass everywhere. "Man, you're wrecking my karma," said a helpful hippie standing by. "I'm going to take my karma and run over your dogma," I remember thinking. Thank you, Ian Black.

Before we left town, we stopped to say farewell to Stephen at the clown camp, where he was spending a week or so. This camp was being run by a group from the Hog Farm, which was founded by none other than Wavy Gravy—the hippie peace activist who got his nickname from B.B. King and was made famous by his appearance at Woodstock ("don't touch the brown acid!"). The Hog Farm was for a time situated outside Taos, and I think it must have been associated with Camp Winnarainbow, Wavy Gravy's California-based operation that still today teaches circus skills to kids. As we gathered to sing together, we realized we were to be led by none other than Mr. Gravy himself, tie-dyed and clown-nosed. "The birds and the bees and the apple trees," we wailed together. Thank god my punk friends couldn't see me then, I thought.

We left the commune, which was a bit north of Taos, and headed to the amazing Chaco Canyon, where we'd spend a few days camping. I remember driving through all these little towns on the way, some of them looking like they were straight out of old westerns, dusty streets and swinging saloon doors everywhere. I also started to figure out some especially annoying car tricks to help us pass the time. My favourite was a manoeuvre I'd do whenever I sat behind the front-seat passenger. If I clicked a lever just right, I learned, the front seat would plummet backwards, and whoever was sitting in it would find themselves in my lap, looking up at my cackling face. At some point, Caroline politely noted that it was no longer funny and I should knock it off. Fair enough.

After camping, we made our way south to Santa Fe. On the way, we stopped to check out a place we'd heard about, a cool cave in a small canyon overlooking the fledging Rio Grande and then, farther along, natural hot springs built right into the famous river itself. As Sunny and I approached the little cave, we noticed someone inside it, sitting cross-legged and chanting, with crystals hanging on strings all around them. We didn't want to disturb the New Age good vibes, so we made our way to the hot springs, which were truly incredible. The thermal water erupted at the edge of the river, and huge stones had been placed in a tub-like shell so that you could relax in the hot mineral water and then instantly cool off by diving straight into the Rio Grande. A few years later I'd conjure this very scene in my first original song, "Five Long Years": "Swimming in the Rio Grande and listening to the Mexican bands singing songs of love, when our hearts were young."

Santa Fe itself charmed me completely. We spent a day wandering around town, and I loved the little health food stores and the cute restaurants and the funky adobe houses. It was quaint and soulful. Sadly, I've never been back, but I hope to get there one day. As we were getting ready to leave, I noticed a poster on a telephone pole advertising an upcoming gig by a band called . . . the Wankers! "These guys actually called themselves that on purpose," I thought, laughing all the way out of town.

We picked up Stephen once his camp was finished and then set out to make our way towards New Orleans, before heading on to Florida. To get there, we crossed the massive bridge that spans Lake Pontchartrain, and I was reminded of one of my favourite songs, Planxty's amazing version of an old folk tune called "The Lakes of Pontchartrain." As always, I was thrilled to actually *be* in a place I'd only heard sung about. It was great, too, to return to New Orleans, three years older than I'd been on my visit with my mom, which meant it was a lot easier to sneak into bars. There were two in particular on my list, clubs I'd heard about again and again as I started to explore the world of blues music more: the Maple Leaf Lounge and Tipitina's, the legendary home of the great Roy Byrd, better known as Professor Longhair. I had great luck at the Maple Leaf, where they knew I was underage but let me in anyway, and I watched the one and only James Booker play piano in the corner by the front window. He wore a patch over his eye, and I couldn't believe I was lucky enough to turn up on a night he was playing; he would die, tragically young, just a few years later. Things were less successful at Tipitina's. The Ackermans agreed to stop in with me, but I was immediately asked for ID. At least I was able to glimpse the hallowed ground inside for a minute before they kindly asked me to leave. I'd play that club a few years later, but back then I felt lucky to get that little taste.

Finally, we made it to Florida and had a nice Christmas on the Atlantic coast in St. Augustine. We even found a scraggly little Charlie Brown–type tree.

On the drive back, we avoided the main interstates in favour of the smaller "blue highways" of the Deep South, passing through Alabama, Mississippi, Arkansas, and Missouri, then making our way through the Dakotas and back to Winnipeg. Here we were, driving through the birthplace of the delta blues and rock 'n' roll that I was now fully committed to, Spanish moss hanging off the trees. I loved the way the blue highways went right through the middle of these little Southern towns. We'd see the people hanging laundry or sipping on a cool drink, languidly lounging on their front porches, watching the cars go by. Many years later I'd borrow the name *Blue Highways* for an album title.

When I finally made it back to Regina, I went through the motions of at least trying to wrap up as many grade ten credits as I could, but really, my Regina time was up. I had to move to Winnipeg.

Sunshine Ackerman lived with her mother and brother in a very cool brick apartment in the Wolseley district of Winnipeg—the top floor of an old three-storey building that once housed a bank. Caroline and Jerry Ackerman had been separated for quite a while by this time and he lived elsewhere. In the apartment, there were two bedrooms, a bathroom, and a quaint living room. It was a place I'd call home for a joyful and industrious year and a half. Sunny and I had so much in common: We'd both grown up in creative Quaker households that shared similar political leanings, and we were both young and filled with a teenage hunger for life. And we were in love, which made things all the sweeter.

I fell in love with Winnipeg too, in a way. It was so much bigger than Regina, and thus it felt as though so much more was possible here. It had been hard to leave home—to leave behind my dad, my friends, my band. But it was time for bigger horizons, and I found them, for a time, in Winnipeg. I settled into a new life and new routines, and Sunshine showed me her Winnipeg and introduced me to some of her childhood friends and inner circle. I hung out a lot in the building's basement, which had a little stereo system and a record player. It was there that I first heard Bruce Springsteen's *Born to Run*, and where I started spending hours listening to records by Otis Rush, Muddy Waters, and other blues greats, deepening my understanding of the music that would define my life.

Because the Ackermans had been friends with our family for so long, living with them in Winnipeg was an ideal set-up and a safety net for a young person heading out on his own. The experience was foreign enough to feel meaningfully different, but familiar enough to not be terrifying. The Ackermans were great, caring people, and I was lucky that they saw in me a kid who needed a change, who would benefit from a fresh start. Caroline was a nurturing, funny woman who looked after us all. She'd gained some notoriety for a cookbook she'd published a few years before, memorably called *The No Fad, Good Food, $5 a Week Cookbook*—a cover worth googling if ever there was one.

I also knew Sunshine's brothers already. Young Stephen lived with us, and the older two were off on their own. Her second oldest brother, Eddie, and I had known each other for years. He'd go on to become a filmmaker, producing strange and funny short films that usually involved animation. I remember one that featured animated dog turds waking up in the spring after the snow melted and having a conversation. But back then, in the late seventies, we just partied. Once, we tried to hitchhike from Regina to Winnipeg, with disastrous results. Our first ride dropped us in a town a few hours outside Regina, where we promptly found a little bar with a Pac-Man machine and wasted most of our remaining money and nearly all the remaining daylight. As dusk gathered, we realized we were in trouble, but we snagged a ride with a religious zealot who was happy to tell us all about Jesus, but also had to drop us in Moosomin, near the Manitoba border, before heading in another direction. Most of the hotels were closed and the ones that weren't didn't want to rent a room to two guys, so there was nothing to do except start walking. At one point we got so tired that we slept in a culvert, ripping up grass and making little beds for ourselves. Around four in the morning we were woken by the sounds of a train slowing down. We emerged from the culvert and saw it in the near distance, now totally still, people walking around it with flashlights as if they were inspecting something. Salvation!

We gathered our modest things and started running towards the stopped train. Just like in the movies, the train began moving just as we got close to it, and just like in the movies, we ran alongside it, desperate to throw our packs up and swing ourselves onto the moving cars. But we were too slow and it pulled away, leaving us dusty and defeated as the dawn broke across the prairies. We started walking again, eventually finding a rest stop where we tried to warm our freezing bodies with a hand dryer affixed to the bathroom wall. As we warmed up, we soon realized that under our clothes we were both completely covered in wood ticks from sleeping in the culvert. We had to strip naked right there in the rest stop bathroom and pluck ticks off each other. When we hit the road again, the sun was fully up, and as we walked east, it burned us both badly. I swear I have lines in my forehead to this day that began on that walk.

When we finally got to Winnipeg, we were amazed to see headlines in the *Winnipeg Free Press* about local anger and protests over a trainload of yellowcake—radioactive uranium that's produced in the generation of nuclear power and weapons. Apparently, the train we almost hopped was hopped up itself! Bullet dodged!

I'd remain friends with Eddie, sometimes hitting the bars with him while I lived in Winnipeg, and I have many fond memories of our hangouts. And, as you'd expect, there are even a few where I don't have any memories at all.

Unlike me, Sunny hadn't dropped out of high school, so while she dutifully attended during the day, I'd roam the streets of Winnipeg, popping into record stores, second-hand clothing shops, and the army surplus. Sometimes I'd wander through the beautifully modern Winnipeg Art Gallery, adjacent to the historic Hudson's Bay department store building. I loved walking the city streets, especially the historical financial district, admiring the beautiful classic architecture of those grand old brick buildings. That was where the legendary Royal Albert Hotel was, a haven for musicians of all kinds, but mostly local rounders and blues players, who would take over the bar on Saturday afternoons for the open mic jams. Local blues heroes Houndog or sometimes Big Dave McLean, who'd been so kind to me over the years back in Regina, would play host. Before long I'd be invited to sit in on a few songs as I slowly made friends around town. I did make one last effort at getting a formal education, enrolling at the Argyle Free School in Winnipeg's north end, which had a reputation for having cool liberal teachers on staff and an alternative approach to learning that emphasized individual freedom as long as you did your work. In retrospect, I think I only did this to make myself feel a bit better about having quit school at home, but it soon enough became clear that music was going to win this battle, and I didn't attend for long.

On our street in Wolseley there was a bulk natural food store and a farm co-op, and these sorts of places opened doors for me too. I met a local blues harp player there who would come into the city from his farm not too far outside town. Directly west of the old bank building where we lived was the Prairie Sky Bookstore, a hippyish place full of New Age music, incense, and books on spirituality. I was still a bit cynical about all that stuff, and I'd make the occasional snide remark, but I'd go in the store, too, and chat with the staff. Sunshine and I would wander around town and hang out, happy to be in love and living this life together.

The biggest issue in my life at that time was a simple one: I didn't have any money. I think my parents may have been sending Caroline Ackerman a bit of cash to help pay for my lodging, but I had no spending money at all, which was hard on a music-loving teenager. I took to playing for change on the streets, mostly on Osborne Street, at a little block of shops and restaurants called Osborne Village. I didn't love busking, but it gave me the pocket money I needed. More importantly, it forced me to learn a repertoire of songs, many of which I could still sing for you today. One highlight was "Riding in the Moonlight," a blues classic written by Willie Dixon and originally made famous by Howlin' Wolf. I was most familiar with the incredible version by John Hammond, and I'd later release it as a single on my *Blue Highways* record. I've played that song almost my whole life, and I love it. I play it with a thumb pick and a heavy, rhythmic thump on the guitar, making the instrument carry both the melody and percussion. People liked that one even then, and I pocketed enough money each time I busked to head to the club and catch some music and have a few beers.

Even back then, I tried to think of my audience, not all of whom want to hear old blues songs. I tried to tuck "Somewhere Over the Rainbow" into each of my little sets, and I remember thinking it was a particularly clever move.

Sometimes, when I was really broke, I'd go to a temp agency. Each day, I'd arrive super early in the morning and register for various hard labour jobs, then go wherever I was assigned. Once, I had to shovel and bag the ashy remains of a house that had been burned to the ground in a major fire, charred plastic and detritus everywhere, not a face mask in sight. That's how people used to roll back then—at least the people who needed the work. Just breathe it in, it will be fine! One time I went to the welfare office to see if I qualified for some help while I got on my feet. The grumpy woman working behind the desk asked me if I had any assets, and when I mentioned owning a custom-made acoustic guitar, she said in no uncertain terms that I should sell it immediately. I did not, and that put an end to that conversation.

As I settled into my new life, I kept returning to the Saturday afternoon blues jams at the Royal Albert Hotel. It's a grand name, but the hotel, especially then, was a dive. People were nice to me, and even though I was underage at seventeen, they'd let me play as long as I hung out in one of the tiny seedy rooms upstairs when I wasn't on stage. This was basically heaven to me, and gave me the opportunity to meet some great and generous players. Brent Parkin was a standout, a local blues hotshot who played B.B. King, Lowell Fulton, and Memphis Slim songs on a gorgeous Les Paul Goldtop with humbuckers. An incredibly talented harmonica player named Gordie Kidder was often hanging around those jams too, and we hit it off. I would go to Gordie's house and listen to amazing blues records by obscure and unknown artists, people like Rosco Gordon, Wynonie

Harris, and Chuck Willis. It was a musical education, and Gordie was generous with his time and knowledge. Years later a lot of that music would find its way onto my Little Big Band record. I was starting to get a reputation around town as a young keener, and after a while I was introduced to a friend of Gordie's named Brian Ellis. Brian was a fair bit older than me, but we got along well, and we started to play as a duo, booking little gigs at coffee shops and local events.

We needed a name, and at that time my favourite record in the world was *Hoodoo Man Blues* by the great Junior Wells, with Buddy Guy playing on guitar. It's a Chicago blues classic, and we took our inspiration from it, christening ourselves the Hoodoo Men. This gave me a foothold in the Winnipeg blues scene—a name to go by, a partner to play with—and soon enough we were booking more and more shows around town. Somebody mentioned that they knew Mitch Podolak, the head booker at the Winnipeg Folk Festival, where I'd gone with my family as a kid each summer, and where I'd seen that James Cotton gig that cemented my dream to be a blues musician. With no small amount of youthful self-confidence, I cold-called Mitch at his office one day, and I was invited to come by for a live audition down towards the end of Osborne Village, not far from where I sometimes busked. I told Brian about the audition date, but he had a working farm south of the city at the time and for whatever reason couldn't make the meeting. I knocked on Mitch's door and made some awkward small talk. He asked me to play a few songs for him, and I nervously fumbled around my now open guitar case, spilling picks and lyric cheat sheets everywhere, and then stumbled through a few delta blues songs, nervously playing guitar and singing. I was sure I'd blown it. Mitch was a kind man with a rough and blunt demeanour and had seen and booked some of the world's best players to this festival. I went home totally dejected.

About two weeks later, I was hanging out in the basement of the bank building, listening to records, when Sunny's mom Caroline shouted down, "Colin, there's a phone call for you!"

It was Mitch Podolak, to my total shock.

"Colin?" he barked.

"Yes, sir!" I said.

"Listen, about your group, about the Hoodoo Men," he said.

He couldn't possibly be calling just to say we were bad, I thought, as I started to feel a flicker of hope.

"Yes, sir," I said.

"Well listen, it isn't much—it's all I can do—but I can book you two for an afternoon workshop slot, just half an hour. Would you be willing to do it?"

"Are you kidding me?" I practically shouted. "Of course we will!"

I thanked Mitch and hung up the phone, pretty much in disbelief, absolutely elated. Later that summer of 1981, when we took the stage at the festival, I wore a buttoned-down shirt, a rarity for me at the time, and I was so proud of my big button that said "Colin Munn, Performer." Brian and I got passes to take the bus back and forth from the site to the hotel where the visiting musicians were staying, we got invited to the parties, we got to hang out backstage. It was an incredible experience for me, being part of that scene, feeling like I belonged.

My mom, Joyce (*left*), and Aunt Arlene in Hope, BC.

My father, Bill Munn.

Me around age three, in Stanley Park, BC. I loved it even then!

Above left: My grandparents Joe and Kay Buck.
Above right: My grandparents' store, Buck's Confectionary, in Hope, BC.

Outside in winter with my preschool pal Kirsten Cameron.

Me on the left, my fellow Eagle Gang members in the middle, unknown boy on right.

With my cousins and siblings on one of our many family road trips.

Munns and Konrads in the Qu'Appelle Valley.

Above: A Munn and Konrad family jam with Robbie on guitar, me grabbing another one, and dad faking a harmonica solo.

Right: My first electric guitar—an Epiphone my parents bought for me at Arcade Music.

Above: Backing Don Freed (*left*) at The Winnipeg Folk Festival, 1983.

Left: On stage The Hoodoo Men at the Winnipeg Folk Festival (1981). Brian Ellis (*left*) is on harmonica.

Right: A poster for a gig of ours in Regina.

Below: On stage with Nick Danger and the Close Calls (a..k.a. the Wankers).

With my friend and sometime roommate, the actor Ian Black.

Uncle Doug with another of his famous Christmas card pranks.

With Stevie Ray Vaughan at his birthday party in New York. Stevie's wearing a Cree medicine bag given to him by my stepfather, Herb Strongeagle.

Our set was fine—my whole family came, and it was amazing to play on one of those small stages in the trees where I'd seen so much magic over the years. But it's backstage I remember most, a mythical place where bluesmen and folk stars roamed, and where I now stood too.

My most memorable encounter was with the great Amos Garrett, a wonderful bluesman who was famous for playing the killer solo on Maria Muldaur's "Midnight at the Oasis." I was a massive fan, still am to this day, and I approached him tentatively to say so at that gig. I complimented him on his rendition of "Dance of the Sugar Plum Fairies," which he'd recorded with Geoff Muldaur just a few years before. He seemed pleased to hear it, and then sat down and taught me how to play it right there and then, like that was the most natural thing in the world. Many years later, Amos introduced me at an event, and mentioned that he'd known me since I was a teenager! Incredible.

The festival slot had been great for my confidence, and the Hoodoo Men started to gather a bit of steam. That year we began playing more shows in Winnipeg, and then farther afield. We were hired to play at a Saskatoon folk club, and we added Regina to our circuit, driving a little triangle among those three cities again and again. In Regina we'd play what the locals called the hippie club. This club was started by most of my friends in Sod Hut and the Buffalo Chips (the goofy band name that I so despised) as a sort of members-only club that allowed for the dispensing of a much-wanted liquor licence. The Saskatchewan Cultural Exchange Society, as it was formally known, was on the second floor of a small building on Broad Street. There was a dance floor in front of the bandstand and, behind that, chairs for around 150 to 200 souls and two shuffleboard tables. Because it was a card-carrying members club, me being underage wasn't a problem.

We also built up our band a bit, and we would always play as a four-piece, adding drums and bass. Our drummer was named Duane Dorgan, a long-haired, somewhat mysterious guy a fair bit older than me, whose house on the outskirts of Saskatoon we'd use as a rehearsal space when we passed through town. On bass was a kid from school named Sid Morgan, who also had played with the Wankers back in Regina. The Morgan and Dorgan rhythm section—what are the odds, I wonder? Duane was big into jazz, and he'd play records for me, records I professed at the time not to like because I thought that made me cool—I was a blues guy, not a jazz guy! I distinctly remember passing judgment on Miles Davis's "All Blues," the track that opens side two of *Kind of Blue*—a record I now love, having come to my senses.

A big early break for us came when we were invited to open for the legendary John Lee Hooker at the auditorium at the University of Regina. I was thrilled to have this chance to see John Lee, and it was made extra special by the fact that my Grandpa Joe and Grandma Kay were visiting Regina from Seattle. You might think I'd be nervous to play in front of someone as esteemed as John Lee Hooker. But those nerves were nothing compared with the ones I felt over playing in front of my famously grumpy grandpa. What would he think of the blues? After all, his idea of good music was Guy Lombardo.

Once we got going onstage, I could tell we were going to be all right, despite my nerves. But as I introduced our fourth song of the set, I dropped my guitar pick. When I bent down to pick it up, I heard my Grandpa Joe's voice rise out of the darkness of the audience and exclaim, "He dropped his pick!" Then he started laughing out loud in the auditorium. Hilarious! Heckled by my own grandpa!

The Hoodoo Men started getting some word-of-mouth momentum in the area, and not long after that, in September 1982, we got a sweet gig, a three-show run opening for George Thorogood in Regina, Winnipeg, and Saskatoon, in big soft-seater theatres. Ian Stewart, mentor to and original member of the Rolling Stones, was playing keyboards for George on that tour. I remember he kept a little bottle of what looked like whisky hidden underneath the keys. One night, I walked up after the show to introduce myself.

"I hear you used to be in the Rolling Stones," I said.

He looked up at me and snarled.

"I was and still am!"

Aside from the financial stress, life in Winnipeg was good to me. I had music, I had my love, and I had a big city to explore. But as so often happens in life, it wasn't to last. One spring, after Sunny and I had been living together for over a year, Sunny's somewhat estranged father asked if we I would be interested in working at a summer camp he owned in Nova Scotia. Sunshine really wanted to go—she was eager for an adventure, and excited about a change of scene for the summer. But I wasn't so sure. Things were starting to come together for me musically, and I wanted to keep chasing that momentum, playing whenever and wherever I could. To me a trip east just sounded like I would be wasting important time away for no real good reason. With this realization, I knew our time together was over. As much as I hated the idea of our relationship ending, I hated the idea of interrupting my musical trajectory even more. Sunny and I would have to split up—there was no way around it. I remember sitting all alone in the upstairs apartment and crying like a wounded animal about the impending breakup. In the end, Sunny headed east to Nova Scotia and I headed back to Regina to plot my next move. It was a beautiful thing we had, and I remain very fond of Sunny to this day. But sometimes life is about moving on.

CHAPTER SEVEN

HOODOO MEN

IT WAS 1982, I was eighteen, and I found myself back in Regina. But this time it felt different. I'd been elsewhere, tried new things, and I knew in my heart that my return to Saskatchewan wasn't a retreat so much as a pause on the way—a moment to collect myself, make a new plan, and take my next steps. I was warmly welcomed by my mom and Herb, who had just relocated back to Regina and bought a house in the south end of town, not that far from my childhood home. They let me crash with them while I figured things out. It was nice to be back with Mom after years of living apart, and I was glad for the opportunity to deepen my relationship with Herb. I started hanging out with my old friends and hustling for gigs with the Hoodoo Men, which had pretty much coalesced into a four-piece group with drums and bass. And I started playing a bit of reggae—why not!—working with a charismatic front man named Frank Carroll who grew up in the Bahamas, claimed to have played with Bob Marley, and had recently relocated to Regina from New York.

Frank called the band Frank Carroll and the Hit Squad, and I loved being with them—there's something about playing blues over a reggae beat that really works. Marley knew this, Peter Tosh knew this—that's why members of the Kinsey family, Chicago blues royalty, appeared on their records and tours. We played Marley and Tosh, along with Jimmy Cliff and others in that reggae tradition, and we rehearsed in the basement of a grand home on Albert Street, a few blocks south of Wascana Lake, where one of our friends lived, a kid named Alex Wilson. Like countless suburban white kids before and after, Alex was what I jokingly called a Waspafarian—crazy about reggae—and he was thrilled to have Frank hanging around his house. They'd make beans and rice together, and Alex would watch us jam. Alex's dad had got remarried to a wonderful woman named JoAnn who would sometimes come downstairs to visit us while we rehearsed, bringing us plates of sandwiches and checking in. Tragically, just a few years later, JoAnn would be murdered. Colin Thatcher, her politician ex-husband, would be convicted of that crime and serve a long prison sentence, though he claims to this day he was framed.

I had fun with the skanking rhythms of the reggae songbook, though I knew it was more of a diversion than my main ambition to play the blues. As I considered my next move, I also kept playing with the Hoodoo Men. We booked shows at the Saskatchewan Cultural Exchange as well as Trifon's Pizza in Regina, and a few bars like Bud's on Broadway in Saskatoon. We'd often book full-week runs, which was a common enough practice back then, though my being underage meant that occasionally a full-week run would end on a Wednesday after I got busted and we got fired; I distinctly remember that happening at Bud's. I made up for it later, once I was properly of age, by playing guitar while walking the length of the bar there during a show, a move that apparently inspired some imitation in the years after, including by Big Dave McLean!

Sometime that summer, I met a Québécois girl named Manon, who was visiting a family friend in Regina. We started hanging out a bit, then started dating more seriously, and that led to a brand new adventure when I returned to Quebec with her that fall. She had to finish her last year of CEGEP, and I decided that it might be an interesting change for me.

When we first arrived in Montreal, I lived in Manon's parents' basement for a short time, in Pierrefonds, west of the city proper. She was from a pretty traditional francophone Catholic family, and while they were welcoming, I could tell they weren't thrilled about the relationship. So soon enough we struck out on our own, moving into a little apartment in Lachine, a borough of Montreal outside the downtown core, not far from the airport. At that time, Lachine was a bit rundown, and our apartment—a tiny, dismal, dark flat with mice everywhere and a pervasive bad smell—matched the neighbourhood vibe. I would light incense to try to improve things, but even that couldn't mask the funk we were living in. We tried hard to make it a home, but we were miserable.

One night, as we were lying in bed, a mouse fell down from god knows where and landed on us, getting tangled in Manon's hair. That was it, we decided, and set about trying to find something better. We ended up getting a place on the ground floor of a three-storey apartment building in Verdun, a nicer part of town that had a pretty little church with two spires nearby, just like the one that inspired the name of the Cathedral district of Regina where I grew up. Rent was higher, but there were no mice. I started busking again, playing guitar for change in the Montreal metro, trying desperately to come up with my half of the rent. My parents sent me a bit of cash a few times, and I applied for welfare and tried to find gigs. But it was hard to break in in Quebec, not least because my French at the time would be charitably described as rudimentary. I found it difficult to make connections in the local music scene, and I felt lonely in this foreign place where I had no friends.

Manon was finishing school, so I'd wander the city, discovering new places, but not having the money to do much of anything. Montreal is built around a beautiful, low-lying mountain that has pathways snaking up it, leading to an iconic illuminated cross at the top, visible from most downtown parts of the city. It was autumn, and the colours were incredible, the leaves on the old trees having turned all shades of orange and red. I'd walk the paths of the mountain, or roam the city streets, and I couldn't help but feel that the turning season matched my turning mood. The days grew shorter, and I grew more homesick. Broke, lonely, and far from home—a challenging combination for anybody, and especially for an eighteen-year-old kid. I even struggled to pay for things at the corner store near us. Because my cash holdings were primarily in the form of nickels, dimes, and whatever else was tossed into my guitar case in the metro, I'd have to count out enough change for a can of tuna, while my neighbours waited in line behind me, as intolerant of my terrible French as they were of how long it took me to pay for anything. I didn't feel good about the situation, but every now and then an extra can of crab-meat would somehow find its way into my pocket during those shopping trips, and I would savour my purloined treasure as if it were the height of sophistication, spooning it out onto crackers for us to enjoy.

I did have one bit of good luck that winter. Concordia University had an open mic contest that paid fifty dollars to the winner of the night's most popular performance. I won on two separate occasions playing the John Hammond version of the Howlin' Wolf song "Riding in the Moonlight." That's a hundred dollars, my friends! At the time of writing, that song is my most streamed Spotify selection with well over four million plays.

In Montreal, whatever money I didn't spend on rent or groceries went to live music, and I did manage to see some amazing shows during my time there. I caught Levon Helm and the Holmes Brothers at a famous club called the Maples, which was in a massive barn adjoining an inn in Pointe-Claire, and which was apparently a fire hazard since it burned to the ground just a few years later. I saw James Cotton again, this time at the little Café Campus club. I'd been a huge fan of his ever since that transformative show at the Winnipeg Folk Festival, and it was amazing to see him in such a different, and much more intimate, setting. As always, he absolutely ripped it up onstage that night.

I spent as much time as I could afford to at the Rising Sun, a bar on Ste-Catherine Street that attracted some heavy hitters, often booking notable American acts for full-week residencies. The club was owned by Doudou Boicel, a Guyana-born impresario who was a key figure in the city's musical scene at that time. He dressed grandly sometimes in a dashiki and matching kufi hat, and kind of held court; years later someone would describe him in the Montreal *Gazette* as looking like an African king. A lot of amazing musicians came through the Rising Sun over the course of its history; Sarah Vaughan, Muddy Waters, and B.B. King all played there. Perhaps because of its diasporic population, Montreal was a hub of jazz and blues, and Doudou held what he called the Rising Sun Festijazz for a few years in the late seventies, which was the precursor to today's world-famous Montreal Jazz Festival.

It was harder for me to find people to play with than it was out west, probably due to the language barrier. At one point I met a harmonica player from San Francisco and tried to work my way into the local scene, but it was a challenge. I found a Saturday blues jam in Old Montreal, and I'd drop in there from time to time. This was a comforting routine, because blues jams transcend language barriers, and it was just like being at the Royal Albert Hotel in Winnipeg—some local heroes, a good harmonica player or two, waiting my turn to go up and run through some standards. Once, to my great excitement, I scored an audition to play for a week at the Rising Sun itself, joining the band of Butch Dixon, one of the many children of blues legend Willie Dixon. At the time, I was playing a Gibson 335 that had been sold to me by a fellow named Roscoe Bell. I would learn later that the provenance of that particular instrument was, shall we say, suspect, but at the time I was blissfully unaware, and I played it with the Hoodoo Men for years. It sounded great, but it came with a massive old coffin-style case, which made lugging it to and from gigs a real pain.

For this particular audition I decided to take with me a Fender Twin amplifier, a famously loud and famously heavy amp that was popular at the time. Depending on what speakers were installed, a Twin could weigh up to eighty pounds. So there I was, lugging an oversized guitar case with a handle that cut into my hand and an oversized guitar amp with a handle that cut into my other hand through the streets of Verdun, onto the metro, soon emerging in downtown Montreal. Unfortunately for me, I emerged a bit too late, and the audition was over by the time I turned up. All I had to show for my efforts were some painful welts on my fingers and palms, and a deepening sense that this Quebec adventure was not quite right for me. I slid further into my funk. Broke and homesick, I felt truly out of place. I remember one particular day I was sitting in a little corner café in Lachine that had jukeboxes at every table. I was gazing out the window on a typical frigid Montreal day listening to Sonny Rollins winding out at the end of the Rolling Stones' "Waiting on a Friend" and realized that it was probably time to head back out west.

About six months into my time in Montreal, a letter arrived that changed everything. It had been sent from Saskatoon to Regina, and then forwarded on to me in Montreal by my mom. It was from a playwright named Ken Mitchell. Ken, along with a musician named Michael Taylor, who played in a band called Humphrey and the Dump Trucks (rivalling Sod Hut and the Buffalo Chips in the annals of bad band names), had written a theatre piece about a washed-up, alcoholic country star. It was to be called *The Laughing Jack Rivers Show* and Saskatoon's 25th Street Theatre company was going to be mounting a production of it for a six-month run. There was a part in the show for a young guitar player, and they wanted me to come out west to audition. They could make no guarantees, and I'd need to pay for my own trip—a tall order at the time, but my mom agreed to help me with the cost of the flight.

It was another quandary. Leaving Montreal would mean leaving Manon behind. I wrestled with the decision for a while, genuinely torn about what to do, but in the end the possibility of a steady paycheque and the lure of something new won out, and I made a plan to head to Saskatchewan and audition. I told myself my trip west wouldn't be permanent, but I think in my heart of hearts I knew things weren't working out for me in Montreal. I think Manon knew that too. As we said goodbye at the airport, we both put on brave faces to hide our sadness. We told each other I'd be back soon, that I probably wouldn't get the job, that this was only temporary. But looking back now, we both knew it was the end. It was lovely while it lasted.

In Saskatoon, I settled into a hotel downtown, my home until the auditions were over and I would discover my fate. I was excited to see some familiar faces after my lonely stretch in Montreal, and among them I was most looking forward to seeing my old Communicart friend Ian Black, who had been cast as the lead in the show I was auditioning for. It was a wonderful reunion—Ian was one of my dearest friends, and we spent our time gallivanting, going out for dinner, staying out until last call, just trying to indulge our shared taste for the good life as best we could figure out in a medium-sized prairie town.

The Laughing Jack Rivers Show was to be directed by a woman named Janet Wright. Janet was extremely direct, very funny, and cursed like a sailor, so naturally I liked her from minute one. She'd acted in a few movies over the years, most notably *McCabe and Mrs. Miller*, starring Warren Beatty and Julie Christie, and much later she would appear in *The Perfect Storm* with George Clooney and John C. Reilly. In Canada, she'd go on to be most famous for her role on the sitcom *Corner Gas*, which was a huge hit, and on which I'd one day guest star. Janet was a dream to work with, especially for somebody as inexperienced in theatre as I was, and I was happy to give myself over to her bossy, seen-it-all charm. I played a few songs from the show on guitar and I read a few lines from the script. I thought the audition went well, and I liked my chances. The next day I got the call: I was right; the part was mine.

When we started rehearsals, I remember wondering how on earth anybody could remember sixty pages of lines. But of course, I already knew the answer to that—repetition, just like I'd done on stages across the west, or busking in subways or on the sidewalk. To learn something you just repeat it, and as you repeat it, you get better. I really enjoyed the rehearsal process, which felt very new to me, even though I'd practised music for most of my life. I had to join the Alliance of Canadian Cinema, Television, and Radio Artists, better known as ACTRA and pay my union dues, which I was happy to do because all of a sudden I was getting paid seven hundred dollars a week for rehearsals and shows. It was more money than I'd ever made before, and I was thrilled by my good fortune and the relative comfort it afforded me. The production team kept me in that same downtown hotel for the three weeks of rehearsals, and when it came time for the show to start, they moved me and Ian to a house that had some connection to the theatre and billeted actors from time to time.

One night, at one or two in the morning, I was doing my laundry in the basement when I heard what sounded like Ian arriving home super late after a night out. I heard the door open and close, then heavy footsteps pounding up the creaky wooden stairs to the second floor of the house. As I folded my shirts, I caught a faint whiff of what smelled like smoke. I left my laundry and headed up to the main floor to see if I could find the source. Once there, it was clear that the smoke was coming from the second floor, which I'd just heard Ian clomping up to.

By this time the smoke had woken others up too. A bunch of us ran up the stairs and stood in Ian's open doorway. He was fast asleep in bed, and the bed was on fire! I shouted his name, but all he did was pull a burning blanket over his head to try and escape the light and noise. Finally, he woke from his drunken slumber and got up, just in time for the rest of us to fling open the window and throw his burning sheets and what was left of his singed blanket out the window. The mattress was smouldering too, and we managed to fold it just enough to cram it through the window, hurling it onto the ground below. It became obvious that an over-served Ian Black had fallen asleep with a lit cigarette. It was terrifying and not the last time I would pull a burning cigarette out of his sleeping hands.

The Laughing Jack Rivers Show was a supper-club type of thing—the audience would sometimes become a part of the show, and scenes would unfold around them as the cast mingled with the crowd. Ian played a washed-up, alcoholic country musician who was trying to keep his life together. I played a young guitar player who wanted to be doing something else entirely. In both of our cases, it was perhaps a bit of art imitating life. Though I was a bit bored in the role, I was having a lot of fun in Saskatoon, and I'd started dating a local actress who was somewhat older than me. And the show was a success, despite its mixed reviews. We made it through the whole six-month run and even took our show on the road, hitting Prince Albert and Yorkton and god knows where else in Saskatchewan. When it was over, I went to Winnipeg for a bit to catch up with my friends, including Brian Ellis, my fellow Hoodoo Man. After a few days, though, I heard that Sunny Ackerman was dating a guy who used to hang out in our neighbourhood when I'd lived there with her, which soured me on sticking around town. So I went home to Regina, where another audition materialized, and I once again found myself onstage in a musical, this one at the Wheatsong Theatre.

While I hadn't exactly loved *The Laughing Jack Rivers Show*, it felt like a masterpiece compared with the cookie-cutter musical I was now cast in. The show, originally called *Toronto, Toronto*, had come out of—you guessed it!—Toronto. But it was written in such a way that, when it toured, it could be reworked to incorporate references to local politics and issues. Thus *Toronto, Toronto* became *Regina, Regina*, though I can't say it was made any better with the changes. Once again I appeared opposite my friend Ian Black in the two male roles. A piano player from Finland was in the mix as well, and we were set for another six months of regular paycheques and eight shows a week. It was becoming a habit, and I was perhaps becoming a bit too comfortable.

At this point I lived in an old CP Rail hotel, now a Delta but back then called the Sask, and I'd hang out with my cast mates and friends in the popular ground-floor bar in the off hours and after shows. When our run was over, I'd just hang around town, complacently passing time, stuck in neutral. I needed a jolt, something to kick my ass into gear. I got one, courtesy of Sandy Cameron, the red-haired, fiddle-playing Communicart impresario who had been such a regular part of my life growing up. We ran into each other one night out on the town and he looked me straight in the eye, one of those looks where you know the person is accessing the very depths of your soul. "What are you *still* doing here?" he asked, and it hit me like a ton of bricks.

Sandy didn't mean what was I doing that night, in that bar. Sandy meant why hadn't I made anything of myself yet, why hadn't I pushed myself towards what I was capable of? I withered under the precision and power of his question. He was completely right. Winnipeg, Regina, Montreal, Saskatoon, Regina again. I was treading water. It was time to start trying to live up to my potential. It was time to make some things happen.

CHAPTER EIGHT

GO WEST, YOUNG MAN

IT'S NOT ENOUGH TO know that you need to get out; you also need to know where you're getting out *to*. And when I reflected on Sandy Cameron's challenge, the path forward became clear pretty quickly. I'd already tried Montreal. I'd spent time in just about every location available to me in the great Canadian prairies. I didn't want to go to Toronto—it might be a good idea business-wise, but I was a west coast guy at heart. When I looked deep into my heart, there was only ever one real option: British Columbia, the stunning province that had captured my imagination since I was a little boy. And more specifically, Vancouver, a city of ocean air and big mountains—a place where I had a sense I might be able to carve out a pretty great life.

The timing was right, as well. My old friend Nathan and his long-time girlfriend Chris asked me and a few other friends from the Wankers if we wanted to drive out west with them. The plan was to stay for a few weeks at somebody's mother's apartment near the airport, in south Vancouver. When we arrived, I was smitten from the first moment I stepped out of the car and into the warm coastal air, blown away by the beauty but also energized by all the exciting things that only a bigger city can offer. Alongside the towering mountains and stunning vistas were hip neighbourhoods, skateboard parks, and clubs where cool bands played every night of the week, as well as big concert venues where global superstars regularly appeared—David Bowie one week, the Clash the next, even the king of pop radio at that time, Michael Jackson. It was a big city, and a music city. But it wasn't just any big city. It was a big city where it never really got all that cold. Having grown up in freezing Regina, this was a major selling point for me. I knew it was the only place for me to live in Canada, and it quickly became my favourite city in the world. It still is, and I've called Vancouver home pretty much since I stepped out of Nathan's car in that summer of 1983.

As our initial two weeks drew to a close, I announced to the group that I had decided to stay on and take a shot at living full-time in Vancouver. Realizing that I would quickly need to make some money now that I had committed to staying, I went down to the Granville Island Market, where I had heard that buskers could open up their guitar cases and play for spare change. Granville Island, if you've never been, is a warren of little streets and alleys full of artisanal shops and galleries, famed in large part for its sprawling indoor market, which is surrounded by benches and picnic tables. It is a place where you can hear buskers all day.

On that afternoon, I scouted for a good spot and asked the friends who were with me to stay close, thinking their presence would give me some courage. But when it came time to play, I realized that all their presence was giving me were nerves; for some reason, I found it embarrassing to be watched by them as I busked for money. So we bid farewell. They headed home, and I headed into my new life.

One slight problem with the new life I was trying to start: I didn't have anywhere to live. Fortunately, Kirsten Cameron, my childhood friend and daughter of Sandy, the very man whose searing question had finally knocked me out of my rut, had relocated to Vancouver as well and moved into an apartment above a framing shop at Main Street and 28th, which was a cool neighbourhood and still is. She offered to let me stay with her for a bit, and I took her up on that kindness without thinking twice. Kirsten also introduced me to some of the local musicians she'd gotten to know, and I started networking and going out at night to see bands at Darby B. Dawes pub, or the Fairview, even sitting in with them every now and then. The Vancouver scene felt vast compared with anything else I'd experienced. But after a few weeks crashing at Kirsten's place, I started to feel bad. I didn't want to overstay my welcome and wear out the generosity of a wonderful old friend. It was time to find my own spot, and find my place in this new scene.

I got a small break from Roger Brant, who had previously been the bassist for the Winnipeg blues band I'd sit in with sometimes called Houndog. He knew a woman who agreed to put me up for a while in her apartment in East Van, and so I couch surfed for a time. Part of the problem, as it so often was in those days, was that I had very little money. I would sometimes work at a car wash, and for a while I got a job moving furniture for the deceptively named Mom's Moving Company—there was no Mom in sight! It was back-breaking work, and it didn't pay much, but I cobbled together enough to get on my feet in this huge new city.

Soon enough, my old friend the musician/actor Ian Black turned up in town. He'd come to Vancouver to audition for a local theatre company, and we quickly started looking for a place to move in and share the rent. You might ask why I'd be eager to move back in with the very man who nearly burned our previous home to the ground by falling asleep while smoking, and that would be a fair question. In response I'd say that I was desperate to get off the circuit of crashing on random couches, and that our friendship trumped the potential fire hazard, apparently. In the end, Ian and I zeroed in on a crummy basement apartment off Main Street, a dark and depressing two-bedroom rental where the tiny windows at the top of the walls offered an endless view of people's passing feet, as if designed to remind you just how far below ground you were at all times. The apartment was sadly also home to the evil and omnipresent cockroach, our constant companion in our dank, dark subterranean cave. But it would be home for now. My old friend and partner in crime was here, and that would dispel some of this new-city loneliness. That counted for a lot during a time of major adjustment.

Once I'd found a literal home, it was time to get more serious about finding a musical one, and I started hanging out at a little club in Kitsilano called Mama Gold's. I was so broke that I'd often walk there, which was a formidable distance. The club became my main hang, a place to meet musicians and show my face in the scene. I'd go see Billy Cowsill or Jim Byrnes hold court. Billy had been in the famous 1960s family band the Cowsills, and sang on hits like "The Rain, the Park and Other Things." He even had a smash hit with his version of the title track from *Hair*, which at the time was one of the biggest musicals in the world. Jim Byrnes was (and still is) an incredible bluesman from St. Louis who played songs by Jimmy McCracklin and James Brown and Al Green. He's also an actor, perhaps best known for his role in the *Highlander* TV shows and some of the *Highlander* movies. Jim and Billy would get me up on stage for a few songs from time to time, and I would surprise everybody by playing the fairly obscure Jackie Wilson song "Reet Petite." Nobody ever expected that song, but it could usually be counted on to bring the house down.

One night at Mama Gold's, I found myself talking to a guy named Willie MacCalder, the super-talented keyboardist for the Powder Blues Band, a big-deal Canadian blues group started by the American-born brothers Tom and Jack Lavin. Their debut record had gone double platinum in Canada, and had won a W.C. Handy Award in the US for blues record of the year. I'd seen them play in Regina a couple of times and it was amazing to find myself suddenly among musicians like them in this magical place. That night, Willie pulled me aside to impart some words of wisdom: "The way you play, you don't have to wait at the back door here to get into this scene. You can walk right through the front door, whenever you're ready." This gave me some much-needed confidence. No matter how broke I was, no matter how hand-to-mouth my life had become, there was a chance that this was a city in which I could make something of myself. And it wasn't just empty advice—Willie was living proof that it was possible. It was a kindness I'll never forget, and exactly the boost I needed.

But whose front door did I want to walk through? There were so many musicians, and so much happening, but one name kept coming up, again and again: David Burgin, a harmonica player from San Francisco (why do they all seem to come from there?), whom I'd met once years earlier when he was playing with the great Amos Garrett. When Amos introduced us, David gave me his number and told me to look him up if I was ever in the Bay Area. Not long after that, I took a spontaneous road trip with my brother Murray, my sister Cathy, and my mom and Herb. I ended up spending a few hours with David when I got to town, and I enjoyed hanging out with him. In addition to being a great musician, he had amazing stories and connections in the music world. He was a very good friend of Junior Wells and also played with a fantastic local slide guitar player named Roy Rogers. Not the cowboy Roy Rogers, but a Bay Area favourite, who is still touring at the time of my writing this book. Sometime after that visit, Dave relocated to Vancouver. We were finally in the same country at the same time, and I really wanted to play with him.

Even before I moved to Vancouver, word had got around that Burgin was going to be putting together a band in his new adopted Canadian hometown, and I became dead set on getting that gig. At the time, everybody in the Western blues scene knew that David's favourite Canadian blues guitarist was Amos Garrett, and if Amos wasn't available, he would use Brent Parkin, the gifted guitar player and front man of Houndog, based out of Winnipeg, and someone I was friends with. But because I was friends with Brent, I was privy to the fact that he was married, and I suspected that, as much as I knew he liked playing with Burgin, he was quite unlikely to disrupt the domestic bliss of his life in Winnipeg to move to Vancouver and play blues shows in nightclubs up and down the west coast. In retrospect, the possibility of playing with David Burgin must have been somewhere in the back of my mind when I decided to extend my two-week Vancouver visit indefinitely. While it wasn't an opportunity I could reasonably have counted on, I think on some level I understood that by sticking around town and making a place for myself in the music scene, I was significantly increasing my odds of being in the right place at the right time.

The gamble worked, and I ended up getting the gig. If you don't know him, David started out in San Francisco, and in addition to playing with Roy Rogers, his distinct harmonica playing was featured on the soundtrack of the iconic film *One Flew Over the Cuckoo's Nest*, as well as on various Charlie Brown cartoons. He was an engaging performer, with a command of the stage that was larger than his medium-sized frame and slight build. He was all about dynamics, and that style of performance was one of David's great fixations as an artist. He always wanted to bring the music to a fever pitch and then on a dime take it way down to a whisper and walk through the audience, playing his harp as the rest of the band chugged along in low gear on stage in support until it was time to go full throttle again. Some years later, after I'd stopped playing with him, I invited him to a gig I had at Boz Scaggs's legendary San Francisco club, Slim's. I was thrilled to be playing there, and excited at the thought of Dave in the audience, seeing how far I'd come since those rough-and-tumble Vancouver days. After the show, we chatted backstage. Did he enjoy the show? Did he like the set list, or my guitar playing? I can't say, because he only had one note: no dynamics! He was probably right—my early gigs could be a bit full-on, a touch too loud—and I'm sure he was frustrated that this obsession he had tried to drill into his band years before didn't seem to have stuck.

To a young me, nineteen or so, freshly arrived in Vancouver, David was an almost mythical figure, and it felt as though there was an element of fate involved with us coming together. This was partly because I'd heard his name whispered reverentially for years. After he'd come to Canada from California, every single musician who saw him was blown away and spoke about David as though they'd seen the second coming of a harmonica god. There was the connection to Amos Garrett—I'd seen Burgin play with him, heard him on Amos's records, and sensed something divine in his harp playing. Because

I needed a mentor, and Dave had a fatherly streak in him, he happily took me under his wing.

We rehearsed in David's East Vancouver garage. The rest of the band included Roger Brant, the former Houndog who had found me a couch to surf, on bass. Drummers rotated a bit, and depending on the gig we'd play with Linsey Umrysh, Chris "The Wrist" Nordquist, or Brady Gustafson. I was very clearly the junior member. But what I lacked in experience I made up for in enthusiasm. I truly couldn't believe my good fortune. The band rehearsed and soon enough started gigging here and there. In Vancouver we'd play a couple of the clubs that hired blues bands, places like the Anchor in Gastown, but more often we'd hit the road to play the odd summer festival or book the Sidetrack Café in Edmonton, while also playing some small bars up the coast in Powell River all the way up to the Yukon.

Through this experience I learned about the disconnect between small communities and the broader music-loving public. While Dave was revered in blues circles, your average Canadian listener had no idea who he was, and so while we never seemed to struggle to book shows, we sometimes struggled to fill the venues. One night that fact combined with another: Dave's mercurial temper. We were playing in Vancouver and there were literally two people in the audience, yet somehow Dave managed to get into a fist fight with one of them. I guess he didn't like a look he was getting or something, and he came down off the stage and got right in this guy's face, telling him that if he didn't want to be there, he should fuck right off. It would have been funny if it weren't so ultimately sad. I'd heard stories about Dave's temper before we started playing together—there was a famous one in music circles involving an altercation between Dave and a bus driver in Winnipeg. But seeing such an outburst in person could be difficult.

Dave's anger would sometimes extend to his bandmates too, if things went bad on stage. I remember one long trip home from Whitehorse after he and Roger had had it out in a big way at the band house while we were in town for a show. Dave had been trying to meditate and quit smoking and drinking on this trip (bad timing, really), and one night Roger and I got in super late from the club. Dave was pissed off and aggressive at Roger and there was a pretty serious physical altercation. Dave slammed Roger into the kitchen cupboards and a very pissed-off Roger grabbed a small Teflon frying pan and brought it down on Burgin's head so hard the pan bent around his cranium.

But despite Dave's anger, there was a tenderness to him too, a vulnerability underneath it all. On that same long trip home from the Yukon, he pretty much cried on my shoulder because things were so rough for him at the time.

I learned so much playing with Burgin, and I'll forever be grateful for the lessons, as hard as they sometimes were to learn. One of the most painful was the lesson that being a musician comes with an almost inevitable share of heartbreak. The whole time we played together, Dave had been slowly working his debut solo record, called *Wild Child*. He'd recorded the bulk of it in San Francisco, for his label

Flying Fish Records. When it was about to be released, a plan came together for a showcase in Vancouver to celebrate the record, one where the label reps would be flying in to attend. This was a thrilling development, because it meant I'd get some exposure to the very people who hand out record deals. Who knows?, I thought to myself. If it went well, maybe I could even end up landing my own contract. A date was set, and I started getting extremely excited. And then one day David took me aside and told me he was going to fly Brent Parkin in for the show—Houndog Brent Parkin, the guy whom everyone had expected him to hire from the start, the guy whose sure-thing gig I had ended up getting. I guess some sure things aren't so sure. Burgin thought I was still too green, and he wanted someone more seasoned for the big night. I was devastated, but I tried hard not to show my extreme disappointment. I muttered something about understanding but went home dejected. I was hurt. More than that, really. I was heartbroken.

I decided I didn't want to be in town when this all went down, so I went back to Regina for a bit to lick my wounds. I thought it would be good to see my parents, and to hang out with my friends and spend some time with my old school buddy Nathan. I stayed with my mom and Herb, and it was great to be back for a bit after a year out west chasing my dreams. I caught up with some people from high school, partied, and had a blast, happy to have been gone but happy too to now be back for a bit, the grand homecoming of a prodigal son. It would turn out to also be one of the luckiest breaks in my life—once again, right place, right time.

One afternoon in June 1984, I rolled into my mom's house and threw my car keys on the kitchen table. I grabbed a mug, headed to the coffee machine, and started to pour myself a cup. Mom and I chit-chatted for a bit, and then she said, "Oh, Colin, someone called for you—they left a number for you to call back, it's on that paper there. He said that you knew him, a guy named Kevin Donnelly?"

I did know Kevin Donnelly. Kevin worked for Perryscope Productions, and he'd been responsible for landing me a couple of really cool gigs in the past. The John Lee Hooker opener, the shows with George Thorogood—those were all thanks to Kevin. Casually curious, I grabbed the phone and called the number. I really couldn't imagine what he'd want with me, especially since I'd been gone for quite a while.

"Hey Kevin, it's Colin Munn," I said, when he picked up after a few rings.

"Colin, great to hear from you, thanks for calling back."

"No problem. So what's up?"

"Listen, I heard you were back in Regina for a bit . . . Could you put a band together to open for a couple important shows by tomorrow night?"

Putting a band together, even in your hometown, is never the easiest task in the world. Putting one together by *tomorrow*—well, it would need to be a pretty sweet gig to work that kind of magic.

"Tomorrow night—that's fast. Hmm, I mean, maybe? It's pretty tight. Where are the shows, and who are they opening for?"

"Have you ever heard of Stevie Ray Vaughan?"

CHAPTER NINE

OPPORTUNITY KNOCKS

HAD I *HEARD* OF Stevie Ray Vaughan?

My pulse quickened as those words sank in. Yes, I had heard of Stevie Ray Vaughan. I'd been watching his ascent for the last year, a legend steadily growing. I'd seen articles about him in *People* magazine. I'd heard the Albert King–esque twang of his Strat on David Bowie's "Let's Dance." And, of course, I'd listened to his music—Herb himself had first showed me the cover of *Texas Flood*, Stevie's masterpiece debut produced by John Hammond Sr., in his car one day. I hadn't just heard of Stevie Ray Vaughan, I *worshipped* Stevie Ray Vaughan. But for now I had to play it cool.

"Yeah, I know who he is for sure," I said to Kevin, the promoter on the line. "Give me a few minutes to make some calls, I'll see what I can put together. Sound good?" My quickened pulse was now a full-on thump, my heart pounding in my chest.

"Sounds good, Colin. Call me back and let me know—but hey, be quick, okay?"

I hung up, briefly panicked, then picked up my mom's phone again and started dialing. First I called my old bass player, Sid Morgan—out of town. I called not one but two of my old Hoodoo Men drummers—no go on either one. What to do now? Inspiration struck and I called my friend Don Freed in Saskatoon, which is where the first of the two gigs was to be. Don was a folksinger, a good one, and he was also a smart and connected guy who could be relied upon to help in a situation like this. (He would also later date Joni Mitchell—accompanying her to my house for that memorable dinner, as you might remember.) He made a few calls and phoned me back, sad to report that he'd struck out too. But he did have an idea—call the Regina Jazz Society, a non-profit promoting jazz in the area, and a great way to connect with musicians. The Society had a couple of names for me, a drummer and a bass player/teacher from a local music store that I could reach out to. These players were a seasoned rhythm section, used to last-minute work and aware and open to the gig.

It was starting to look like we had a band, so I called Kevin back and told him it was all set, no problem, things would be great, nothing to worry about, and that I'd see him in Saskatoon. Then I remembered to ask what time should we arrive and could we have a space to have a quick rehearsal? I hoped this last question didn't set off alarm bells for Kevin. Then I hung up and started to worry about how this group of musicians who'd never even met would suddenly be worthy of opening for the great Stevie Ray Vaughan the very next day. I threw some clothes in a bag, grabbed a guitar, and left town first thing the next morning in my mom's aging grey Valiant. This was a mostly trustworthy car that she would lend me from time to time when I was home. Or at least it was trustworthy until you went over railway tracks or bumps of any kind. That would send the wheels shaking for half a minute until it subsided. All part of the fun! Saskatoon, here we come.

Kevin had told me to show up at the Centennial Auditorium no later than 5 p.m. When I pulled in, well before the allotted time, I saw Stevie's tour bus parked outside. I had never seen a tour bus up close before, and the fact that Stevie could be in that very bus, or in the building I was about to walk into, really floored me. I waited around the back entrance of the auditorium, eager to meet my new bandmates, and eventually a small white pickup truck found its way to the loading bay, a jumble of drum hardware and a bass amp loaded in the back. In the truck was drummer Gary Arnush and bassist Tim Krieser—each twenty or so years older than me, but hopefully their experience would mean they had the chops to get us through the challenge of playing the set ahead of us. Though there was a slight confusion about exactly what challenge we were facing: As they pulled up, they asked if we were playing a wedding in the banquet hall! I said no, we were in the big room, and were opening for the one and only Stevie Ray Vaughan. As we shook hands, I realized we had to be on stage in less than three hours.

Stagehands led us into the building, where they had set up a small, improvised rehearsal space in a backstage room. The promoter had arranged for a backline Fender Deluxe Reverb amp and a couple of cables for me, which were waiting there, and I opened my lone Ibanez guitar case and tuned up. We'd only have time for a quick practice, so I'd been thinking about simple blues we could manage with scant preparation. On the drive I'd run through options in my mind. We needed about thirty-five minutes of music, and I was thinking about Big Bill Broonzy's "Key to the Highway" and Willie Dixon's "Seventh Son." As we started up, I could tell that the drummer and bassist could manage a decent shuffle, which is always a good sign.

When we were about three songs into our little practice session, the door burst open, and in it stood the cowboy-hatted, boot-wearing Stevie Ray Vaughan himself. It was like the world stopped right there. And we did too, cutting whatever song we were running and just staring at the door frame, like god himself had dropped by to check on us.

"Is it true what I heard?" Stevie asked, looking straight at me.

"I don't know," I said. "What did you hear?"

"I heard y'all just met and you've never played together before." This, and everything else he said, uttered in his lazy, charismatic Texas drawl.

My heart was in my throat. This was the guy I'd been listening to constantly, the wizard who channelled Albert King and Jimi Hendrix and Buddy Guy all at once, who had distilled the best of the greats while adding his own spectacular voice, taste, and energy to the mix. He was a modern blues genius, and he was standing in front of me, asking if it could possibly be true that these three guys who were going to open for him had only just been introduced. God, I thought, he's probably pretty unimpressed with this situation!

"I'm afraid so," I sheepishly admitted, and Stevie burst out laughing! A huge smile broke out across his face, and off he went, confident that we'd figure it out. We ran through a few more songs—a couple of Little Walter numbers, and Jimmy Reed's "Baby What You Want Me to Do"—and we started to find our groove. If Stevie found this all so funny, I reckoned, maybe it would all turn out okay.

When I look back on that night now, I see that everything I had done up until that point had led me to this moment. Every artist I had seen play, every record I listened to over and over again to get that one lick. Every show I had agreed to play no matter how apathetic the audience, every crappy bar booking I fought through for a whole week. All the things I did without really knowing where they'd lead me, while thinking I'd just do them until something changed and all of it made sense. This was it—this night was it. Everything aligned, and nothing was ever the same again.

As we stood backstage, ready to go on, I was overcome with nerves. There were well over two thousand people out there, one of the biggest crowds I'd ever played to, and I'd known my bandmates for just a few hours. I tried to steel myself, tried to stay calm, but it was an uneasy situation. We had no crew, so we were pretty much on our own, and we didn't even have the particular camaraderie that arises from having played together to fall back on if we got in trouble during our set. But the show must go on, no matter how nervous the nineteen-year-old front man is, and so we took the stage.

I counted off a simple blues shuffle in E, the Jimmy Reed song we'd run through backstage, and we settled into the groove. We did a passable job. As the song wound down, we breathed a collective sigh of relief and tore into our second number, "Hoodoo Men Blues," the Junior Wells classic that I'd named my very first band after. It was also a minor victory—the crowd was warming up, starting to come alive, and we were, dare I say, beginning to crush it a bit. It was happening, and it was going just fine. We were going to make it.

Or maybe, just maybe, we *weren't*. As I launched into a solo in our third song, I felt the telltale snap of my high E string breaking. Not ideal, but adrenalin was on my side, and you can adapt—it makes things a bit harder, and you've got less fretboard to work with, but you can survive a solo without that high E. I kept going, trying my best to pull something special out of the Ibanez Artist that I played at the time (because Amos Garrett played one). These thousands of people in front of me had paid good money, and my hero might just be listening backstage, so I gave it my best shot.

I worked through a few more bars, and then true disaster struck: My G string broke, and the guitar was instantly unplayable. It wasn't just a matter of being down two strings at that point. When the

G string breaks, the entire tension of the guitar shifts, and every other string goes terribly out of tune, making things absolutely untenable. There was nothing I could do. The band kept playing, locked in the groove, and I walked to stage right and stood behind the PA stack, totally lost. In addition to having no crew, I had only this one guitar. I was royally screwed.

I looked across the stage and locked eyes with a member of Stevie's crew, who, miraculously for me, turned out to be René Martinez, Stevie's wizard guitar tech. René disappeared for a second and then emerged again, walking towards me across the stage with an Olympic white Strat loaded with Danelectro lipstick-tube pickups—one of many iconic Stevie guitars, known as Charley, after Charley's Guitar Shop in Dallas, where it originated. Rene looked me in the eyes and, with sympathy and understanding, handed me the guitar, saving the show and saving my ass . . . almost. I say almost because at that point in time I didn't yet know that Stevie tuned all his guitars a half tone down so he could still bend the heavy strings he liked, so when we struck up our fourth song, I was in a different key from the bassist! He figured it out fast enough and were on our way, finishing the set with all strings intact and all songs performed in the same key. The crowd seemed into it, and we walked off stage feeling a lot better than I had feared we might.

I took a breather in the dressing room and then went and stood side stage and watched Stevie and his band Double Trouble tear that place into tiny little pieces. I couldn't believe my good fortune, watching the performance up close. I had a massive grin on my face as Stevie played the last song in the set. When he was done, he came off stage right, just where I had been standing, hoping not to be in the way.

"Hey man, want to come play a song with us?"

Are you kidding me?!

So that's how I ended up on stage with Stevie Ray Vaughan and Double Trouble on the very first day I met them. We played "Pride and Joy" and "Love Struck Baby" and something else I can't remember now. I played for three songs in a row and Stevie gave me tons of room for solos, and as the last song of the jam finished, I started to walk off stage, beaming, when all of a sudden a large hand grabbed mine and pulled me back for a final bow. We went back to our dressing rooms and my one-gig-only band and I talked about how wild this whole thing had been.

If you'd asked me the next morning, I very well might have said it had all been a dream. But it wasn't—I awoke to a review of the show in the Saskatoon *StarPhoenix*. They got the name of the band wrong, mistaking us for Toronto's the Dice, who had opened the show the night before in Edmonton. They got my name wrong, calling me Dice front man Gary Lima. (They weren't the only ones who made that mistake. The next morning before we left town, I was walking across a bridge and someone yelled, "Hey! Gary Lima!" from a passing car.) But it didn't matter. It had happened, and it was going to happen again; the seeds of so much had been planted, though I couldn't have known it then. We headed south to play Regina, the hometown I'd left just two years before to try to make it on my own out west.

I drove the three and a half hours to Regina in an excited haze, and by the afternoon I'd settled in back at my mom's house with my friend Don Freed, who'd come down with us from Saskatoon. Sound check wasn't until 5 p.m., so we killed some time and hung out. My mom and Herb knew that something pretty special had happened the previous night, and the infectious energy was still coursing through my veins.

The show was booked for the Saskatchewan Centre of the Arts, a venue I knew well. I remembered being less than five years old when it was under construction. Our family would drive there and watch it being built—cranes and bulldozers and heavy machinery, eye candy for a little kid, as I watched a future I didn't know I'd be lucky enough to have being erected right there. While near the site, I somehow dropped an errant drill on my foot one day in 1969, and I still have a small mark where its bit pierced my skin. In other words, I had come up alongside this building, and I had a connection to it. I'd seen a lot of shows at the Centre of the Arts over the years, too. The first band I ever saw there was the Canadian band Chilliwack. I remember watching Bill Henderson and thinking it must be incredibly cool to front a rock band. Later, I saw Taj Mahal, Goose Creek Symphony, and the Police. I was excited, sure. I was nervous, naturally. But most of all, I wanted to do right by Stevie, and to do so in front of my hometown crowd. My family would be there, including my brother Robbie, my hero as a kid, whose left-handed guitar I played the first time I ever picked up the instrument. My high school friends would be there. And I knew the house would be full of the musicians I'd come up alongside, the people who'd taught me, mentored me.

That night I got a lucky boost from Stevie. The guys and I headed to the Centre of the Arts and got up on stage for sound check, running through a few numbers to make sure everything was sounding good. Now that the band had played a show together, we knew we would be slightly tighter tonight and that we could relax a little bit. After sound check, I got talking to Stevie (still unable to believe I could do something as casual as *talk* to Stevie Ray Vaughan). We hung out side stage, and even played a bit of guitar. As we talked, he reached into his pocket and took out a small, worn leather pouch. I think he must have known I was still nervous.

"Hold on to this for a minute or so," he said. "It'll help."

"What's this?" I asked, taking it into my hands.

"That? That's a mojo hand."

I'd heard of this thing called a mojo hand in blues songs for as long as I could remember. But I didn't really know what it was until that moment, when I was holding one. I would read up on them later. They're good luck charms, basically, in the African American spiritual tradition of hoodoo, which, of course, intersects in some big ways with the blues, as you might imagine based on the name. They're pouches, sometimes flannel, often leather, containing magical items like John the Conqueror root, and they're often believed to contain particular spirits. I don't know how Stevie came into possession of his, but he was sharing it with me as a blessing of sorts, I felt. Hold on to it for a minute and its power would enter me. It was his way of saying everything was going to be okay.

As I handed it back to him, I couldn't resist asking an Albert King–related technical question about five-fret string bending, a tricky move that Albert did, and that Stevie could do too; it was key to a lick I'd heard a million times but never quite been able to get my head around. Stevie patiently answered me, talking me through it, and then, guitar in hand, played the King riff I couldn't manage. I watched in reverent silence.

"Could you do that again, please," I asked, needing to see it a few more times for its technical ingenuity to sink on.

"Nope, that's all you get!" he said with a laugh, as he headed off to run his own sound check.

That night we played better than we had in Saskatoon. Maybe it was the saxophonist we'd added, a revered Regina jazz player named Arnie Davis, who was a great fit. Maybe it was the mojo hand. Or maybe I was supercharged by the familiar faces in the crowd. Mostly it was that we'd actually had a chance to gel just a tiny bit, and I didn't break any strings. We ripped through our set in the high-energy auditorium, and I was proud of our playing, and proud to be there.

Backstage that night, in between our opening set and Stevie and Double Trouble's main act, the band and I were hanging out in our dressing room, basking in the glow of a job well done, or at least well enough done. I was hyped up still, full of adrenalin, high off the thrill of sharing a stage with my all-time favourite player. And as I often do when I'm feeling energized, I started singing. That night it was Ray Agee's version of the song "Tin Pan Alley." Stevie must have been passing by at exactly the right moment—he heard it, stopped, and walked into the little room.

"Colin, what was that you were singing?"

"Tin Pan Alley," I said.

"Right, but . . . that was Ray Agee's version," Stevie said. "You know Ray Agee's version?"

Ray Agee was a virtually unknown Alabama-born, California-based blues and R & B singer, one of these guys who recorded a ton of music but in relative obscurity. I loved his singing, and especially his version of "Tin Pan Alley," which he'd cut in the sixties.

"It sure is, Stevie," I said.

"You're telling me someone from here," by which he meant *Saskatchewan*, "somebody from this place knows about Ray Agee?"

"Absolutely!" I said. "Ray Agee does the best version of that song, apart from yours, of course."

Stevie was delighted, and we settled into one of those kinds of nerdy conversations that musicians sometimes have. We talked about Otis Rush and Jackie Wilson, and compared notes on some of our favourite blues guitar players and singers. A real friendship was formed right then and there, in that moment of shared appreciation for this musical tradition we were both trying to honour, in our own way. It was a friendship that would change my life, sending me down the road I was finally ready to take. But in that moment, it just felt like a joyful connection with a kindred spirit. And soon enough, that kindred spirit needed to take the stage.

That night I found a place near the guitar stands on the side of the stage to watch Stevie's show. He and the band absolutely killed it, as always. The thing I remember most was how *loud* it was. The stage had been set up with Plexiglas baffles in front of the amps, a conscientious way to try to keep the levels manageable in the acoustically perfect venue. But halfway through the show Stevie called for them to be taken down, and it was all-out mayhem, the glorious noise of one of the world's best bands playing as hard and as loud as they could. That night Stevie played guitar behind his back. He played guitar with his teeth. And when he played his beautiful instrumental "Lenny," he sat at the edge of the stage, his legs dangling, and you could have heard a pin drop. He basically slaughtered the good, blues-loving people of Regina, and I bet every single person who was in that room will remember that night for the rest of their life.

At the end of the show, Stevie walked off stage and again asked if I'd join in for an encore. I'd hoped this would happen—of course I did!—but I hadn't wanted to presume. He said they'd play one number then he'd signal for me to come out, and when he did, I was once again in heaven. We played "Texas Flood" and "Love Struck Baby," and when we were done, I started to walk off stage to give the band the space to say good night to the crowd. As I did, I felt a massive hand grab my arm and hold on tight, pulling me back out. What a gesture, what a night. We all took a bow together.

Afterward, we hung out on the bus with Stevie and his band and crew, parked outside the Regina Inn. We somehow ended up at a well-known live music venue called the Paddock that was owned by one of my school friends' dad. We all arrived at the club in Stevie's bus and parked in the lot in the back. There was a fairly beaten old National steel guitar kicking around the backstage lounge and the word was that it used to belong to the great Big Bill Broonzy, whose song "Key to the Highway" I'd played both nights opening for Stevie. It felt like a sign of sorts. Performing that night was a ZZ Top cover band, and Stevie ended up onstage, surprising and delighting the audience by sitting in on some tunes. Don Freed and I stayed up until five or six in the morning, waiting for the next day's newspaper to come out, before heading back to my mom's house to crash.

We finally got our hands on the day's fresh *Leader-Post* and we got a pretty good review. The writer, Bruce Johnstone, had some kind words for my guitar playing, and appreciated that the band was as tight as it was, especially given it was only our second performance together, which he noted. But I was happiest to see the way he acknowledged Stevie's grace in supporting me. "Perhaps the ultimate proof of Vaughan's greatness," Johnstone wrote, "is that he unselfishly brought Munn on stage for the encore. In a business where bloated egos are the rule, rather than the exception, it's a pleasant surprise to see an established star share the spotlight with an up-and-comer, like Munn." I couldn't have said it better myself.

After we read the review, we headed home. I must have fallen asleep in the passenger seat, to be woken by water being sprayed on me by some sort of sprinkler that Don, ever the practical joker, had managed to turn on inside my mom's car. It was an absurd and fitting end to a ridiculous, whirlwind adventure. Later that day Stevie asked if I wanted to come play some more shows with him in the US. I wanted to, of course, but I didn't have a regular band. I phoned David Burgin in Vancouver to suggest that we do the shows together, but Dave said he couldn't. I even told him that if he wanted to call the band the David Burgin Band, that was fine with me, I just wanted to continue this ride somehow. But Dave was firm, he couldn't do it, no matter what we called ourselves. Now I had a dilemma on my hands, torn between two important figures in my life, and unsure of how to proceed. These past few days were going to profoundly shape my story, but maybe not right away.

CHAPTER TEN

MENTORS

I PICKED BURGIN, as crazy as it might seem. And about six weeks later I found myself in a hallway at the oddly round Chateau Lacombe hotel in Edmonton, guitar in hand, as I waited for my current band leader David Burgin to knock on the door in front of us. It's a door we had to knock on, but one I wasn't necessarily prepared for. That's because on the other side of that hotel room door was a challenge, one I was thrilled to have the opportunity to face, but also one I was daunted by. So many of life's great moments have that combination, don't they? That day, on the other side of *that* door, was Dr. John, the piano-playing legend from New Orleans, the internationally renowned powerhouse behind such hits as the ultra-funky "Right Place, Wrong Time" and the sublime "Such a Night." He was in town to appear at the Edmonton Folk Festival, where he planned to take the stage with the great Maria Muldaur. The pair had been a late booking to fill in for two cancellations, Bo Diddley and a talented Cape Breton musician named John Allen Cameron. I was in town to play the same festival, on the bill for an afternoon slot with David Burgin and the Nightshades, but it looked as though we were going to also be the last-minute backup band for the last-minute headliners. Fate has its way again!

For me personally, it was a huge deal. I'd returned to Vancouver from my gigs with Stevie and rejoined the Nightshades, easing back into things with David, still feeling a bit hurt by how everything had gone down earlier in the summer. But here was a chance to play a festival I loved, and in support of musicians I admired.

When I was growing up, Maria Muldaur had been in regular rotation on our family's turntable. I remember singing along to "Midnight at the Oasis" as a kid, and as I've mentioned, the killer solo on that song was played by my early hero Amos Garrett. The year before, Maria had released a jazz record called *Sweet and Slow*, which I'd really enjoyed. And who played piano on that record? None other than Mac Rebennack—or at least that's how they credited Dr. John on the liner notes, using his given name. So when word came down that we'd be backing them on short notice, I naturally turned to that record to start to prepare. I already knew it a bit, which made things a little easier, though I was not then (and still am not) a jazz player in the strictest sense of the word. But I did my best, listening to the record a few times and picking things up as well as I could. It's crazy to think about, but I was just twenty years old, anxiously practising, doing my best to get ready for an unknown assignment with these music giants. Don't forget, in these days you couldn't just search any song on iTunes or Spotify—that kind of immediate access was still a long way off.

Leading up to the gig, I bugged Burgin constantly, asking if he'd heard anything about the set list, or even just a sense of a general direction for the show. I started to have a gnawing feeling that even though my practising *Sweet and Slow* was the obvious thing to do to prepare, it might not end up being that helpful. Eventually, Dave heard back, and my sneaking suspicion was proven right: We wouldn't be playing *anything* off that record; instead, we would be dialing up a set featuring the hits and a bunch of other raucous crowd-pleasers I did not know the first note of. And so it was at that point we found ourselves rushing to the hotel, where we'd been promised a meeting with the great man himself, one I desperately hoped would shed a little light on the assignment ahead of us.

After some time, we knocked on that hotel room door and someone answered, ushering us into a totally dark room—the blinds were drawn, and the only light came from that blazing seam that forms around hotel curtains when they're closed on a sunny day. Dr. John himself was in bed. Whether he was sleeping something off or just sleeping in, I don't know. There was a rumour at the time that he was on methadone to recover from a heroin addiction, but I couldn't say for sure that it was true. He handled the intrusion gracefully—he had, after all, invited us over—and after a few pleasantries I was able to make my confession: I'd learned the wrong material, and I was totally unprepared. To his credit, Dr. John didn't seem too bothered by this. In fact, instead of panic on his face, there was a note of amusement. He reached out and grabbed my guitar and proceeded to play the changes right there, as I hovered at the edge of his bed.

It was hot that weekend, August 1984, and when the Nightshades played our afternoon set, we all wore shorts, which is mortifying in retrospect—there are Blues Rules for a reason! But by the time our evening slot with Dr. John and Maria rolled around, things had cooled off slightly into one of those perfect Canadian summer nights where everybody in the crowd feels grateful to be alive and outside as the stars emerge. I was out of my depth, and I knew it even then, but that's what it is to apprentice as a musician. Sometimes you're out of your depth and it feels awful. But sometimes you're out of your depth and it's magical, you're right there on the edge, fighting to keep up, fighting to make your fellow bandmates proud—and, in this case, fighting to make a few living legends proud. Those are the moments where you grow, and I definitely did that night.

In a way, it felt like being onstage with Stevie, at least insofar as you couldn't have wiped the smile off my face if you tried. Dr. John growled out the blues, lacing every song with his sinuous, unforgettable keyboard lines. Maria Muldaur shimmied and swayed and crooned in her distinct, evocative voice. And I looked out at the crowd, grateful and inspired, determined not to lose touch with either of those feelings. We played "Such a Night" and it truly was. In my heart I knew it was one I'd never forget. Even the stage lights could not obscure the silhouette of the moon and the star-studded sky.

While it was nice to be back with David and the guys for a bit, I knew my time with the band was winding down. Partly it was that I might never get over the hurt of getting the boot for Dave's record-label showcase, even though that had led to a life-changing opportunity for me with Stevie. But it was also just time—things run their course, and I think I'd known it was getting near the end even before I was temporarily replaced. If I'm being honest, the end probably came around the time a hungover Dave cried on my shoulder on the long flight back from our disastrous and strange trip to the Yukon a few years earlier. So once we got back to Vancouver from Edmonton, I wrapped things up and made the decision to move on. I wouldn't end up needing to move far.

I'd first seen Billy Cowsill play at Mama Gold's, the great little Vancouver club I frequented whenever funds allowed. Billy had initially gained notoriety as part of the Cowsills, a family band from Rhode Island in which he and five of his siblings had basically been a real-life version of TV's Partridge Family. Like so many wholesome things that were successful, they ended by becoming something of a joke as the hippies and hipsters took over the sixties. Billy spent the seventies playing all over America. In 1975 he quit the Cowsills for good and escaped the fickle LA music scene to disappear into

Canada—to Yellowknife first, then Edmonton, and finally Vancouver, where he would quietly settle into the local music scene, a really cool guy with a super-cool story and a voice for miles and miles. He was well-known and well-liked by local musicians, and he filled his sets with what he called "dead guy music"; songs by Ricky Nelson, Elvis Presley, John Lennon, the Yardbirds, Buck Owens, and Don Gibson were in his fairly wide repertoire. He took me under his wing and invited me into the musical fold. It was a simple band—upright bass, two guitars, and drums, with Billy singing lead, and backup vocals from me and the bassist, Elmar Spanier—and I absolutely loved being part of it.

Billy had a truly unique voice and persona. It's hard to describe it except by saying he was the real thing, which is an overused expression, to be sure, but in this case perfectly apt. Totally authentic. There was something about him, a kind of mystique, perhaps stemming from his having been in a commercially successful band and then living to see that same success become a weight around his neck. He'd grown through that journey, learned some things, and he understood something about life and art in a way that was truly mature and clear-eyed. It gave him a presence, on and off the stage, and when he played and sang, he was doing it for himself. Also to pay the rent, sure, but playing every night in a bar won't get you fame and fortune. But he'd had that, and now he did this; Billy knew his art, and that his art was his truth, and he worked to honour that. For me, he became a role model. He cared about me, and I cared about him, and I was lucky to be there with him, learning from him, continuing to grow into the musician I am today. Billy was one of only three people in my life who affectionately called me Colly. He died in 2006, but I can still hear him calling me that in his distinctive voice.

I was with Billy and the Trainwreck, as we were called, for a few years off and on in the mid-eighties. We'd play almost entirely in western Canada, especially in Calgary, where we had a reliable following. I loved this arrangement—I didn't have the responsibility of my name on the marquee, of being the draw, and so I didn't have the crushing disappointment if the house wasn't full. I couldn't have known it at the time, but it would basically be my last regular gig as a sideman, as part of someone else's band, and when I look back on it now, I'm pleased to remember that I appreciated the freedom that gave me at the time. Sometimes you don't realize the gifts of such situations until after the fact, but I knew how good I had it, and I loved playing with those guys. I showed up, played guitar, sang my backup parts, and that was it. But as carefree as it was for me, I'm sure it was hard on Billy, leading a group while managing everything that goes along with it. I remember a few times when he got into it with club owners who wanted an extra set. Maybe Billy didn't like the guy's attitude, or didn't like the way he'd asked. Sometimes he'd even quit the gig before it began, though even then he always looked after his band members. Once, after he bailed on a job that cost us a week's worth of work, he paid me for the lost time by giving me a Fender Twin amp.

In July of '85 we booked an especially sweet gig, opening for k.d. lang at the Crystal Ballroom in the historic Palliser Hotel in Calgary.

Billy and k.d. shared a manager, a guy named Larry Wanagas, who'd booked us for the gig, doubtless eager to attach Billy and the Trainwreck to the coattails of his rapidly rising star, k.d. It was a great show and it was so exciting to see how Kathy Dawn Lang commanded the stage from start to finish in the way only k.d. can. Something to see. A few years ago a limited edition vinyl run of our opening set was released, but I asked them to omit the songs I sang in the set. To my ears, I sounded too green. I was still settling into my voice and, rightly or wrongly, I didn't want those tracks out there for all to hear. The rest of the record is a great listen, though, and it was fun for me to momentarily relive that special night playing with my friend Billy Cowsill and the band.

Later that week, that same Larry Wanagas asked me for lunch at that same Palliser Hotel, so he must have seen something he liked during the gig. I was thrilled to be sitting down with a real talent manager like Larry. He told me he was planning to relocate to Vancouver, and that he'd be partnering there with another manager named Steve Macklam. Larry asked me if, once the move was done, I'd be interested in being managed by him and Steve. I didn't yet know Steve, but I did know he'd been instrumental in getting k.d. a deal with the US label Sire Records, run by the infamous impresario Seymour Stein, the very man who'd signed the Ramones, the Smiths, Talking Heads, and many more. So even though I didn't know Larry's soon-to-be partner, I was *very* interested, and I told him as much. I left that lunch meeting feeling that some things might be on an upswing—that all this cavorting about in pubs and bars might lead to something after all.

I played with Billy for the rest of that summer until one day, hanging around my East Vancouver apartment, I received another one of those lightning-bolt phone calls from a promoter. Could I get to Edmonton and Calgary in the next couple of days to open some shows for Stevie, who was beginning a Western swing of dates? I paused to wonder how on earth this guy had tracked me down out here in Vancouver, and then quickly moved on to wondering how on earth this miracle could be happening again!

After I put the phone down, I looked at my roommate Doug with big, imploring eyes that said, "Could we, pretty please, drive your little pickup truck across the mountains to Alberta?" Doug was a great friend and only needed to think about it for a few minutes before saying that he was up for it as long as he could book the days off work. He started figuring that out, and I got on the phone to once again conjure a band out of thin air to open for my hero Stevie, the world's greatest blues player. I asked some connections in Edmonton for names for a rhythm section and hired a sax player named Dave Babcock, which would allow me to throw some solos his way. Doug got the time off, we packed some suitcases, and we left Vancouver around noon, a twelve-hour drive in front of us. Or really, since I didn't have a licence at the time, a twelve-hour drive ahead of poor, generous Doug.

Things went well enough for the first while. We were excited, and we chatted and enjoyed the mountain drive. Around 9 p.m., we hit the iconic town of Jasper, Alberta, and grabbed a late dinner and some gas before proceeding on with the final stretch of the journey. Soon, Doug started struggling to stay awake, so my job became keeping him engaged in conversation. After a while, though, conversation wasn't enough—Doug's eyes would get heavy midway through a sentence—and we both knew we'd need more. So we did what people always do to stay awake on a long drive—we put the windows down. Even though it was August, it gets cold in the mountains at night, and soon enough we started to think we were more likely to freeze to death than die in a sleep-induced accident. After some time, the mountains finally gave way to the prairies and the lights of Edmonton appeared in the distance. We knew we were going to make it, and we checked into a cheap motel in the early morning to sleep off the epic drive.

I'd arranged to meet my new band at one of the members' house at 2 p.m. for a quick rehearsal, and as soon as I woke up, I started to get that queasy, nervous feeling that comes ahead of a big gig. I shrugged off the nerves, but right behind them was another feeling, something like a mild cold—perhaps the result of exhaustion, or perhaps from our overdosing on freezing mountain air the night before. I shrugged it off too, since nothing was going to get in the way of my reunion with Stevie. I met up with the new guys, and we settled in quickly enough. I was very glad to have the saxophone player on board, since it gave our band a similar configuration to the one John Hammond used on the records that had been so influential in my development.

We headed down to the Jubilee Auditorium, and I wrote out a set list for the night. Around that same time I felt the beginnings of a sore throat, and I started getting a bit hoarse—nothing cough syrup couldn't cure, I thought, and countless bluesmen before me had had more than a touch of rasp in their vocals. I kept up enough energy to take the stage with my new band, and we were quite good that night. I didn't break a single string, and we turned in what the *Edmonton Journal* would the next day call "a bruising half-hour of obscure blues-rock nuggets." We were warmly received by the crowd, and in that review too, where the writer praised the broad grins we all exchanged on stage. She said I reminded her of Buddy Holly in look and voice! Hey, take what you can get, right?

Stevie and I caught up after our set, and he asked me if I'd like to sit in with Double Trouble during the encore—this was to be one of those nights. I said yes, naturally, and Stevie proceeded to destroy the audience the way he always did, with that perfect combination of muscle and soul that made him the best. Watching him in those years felt somehow divine; it was as if some god were speaking, some greater force moving through his mind and into his fingers to create this superhuman music. When Stevie played, a portal opened through which he could channel all the greats who'd come before him while still sounding totally, absolutely, completely like himself. I watched, as usual, from the side stage, as Stevie pushed the songs past anything you could ever expect from them, into the sublime.

When he was done, I got swept up in the group as they headed to the dressing room for a quick breather before the encore. Stevie signalled for me to come along, as if to discuss song selection for the encore, and before I knew it, I'd followed him into the back of an unused dressing room where two unbelievably long lines of cocaine were waiting for us on a mirror. He handed me a rolled-up dollar bill and motioned for me to go ahead and snort one of them. I'd done coke before, but nothing like this quantity. I had to take a break half-way through the line and regroup before polishing it off. Stevie did his in one long, fluid snort, then told me he'd call me out after the first encore. I sat there in the dressing room, basking in the glory of the moment, and suddenly very high. And then, just as suddenly, very sick; it turns out I'd reached my limit when it came to the white stuff, especially when suffering from a minor cold. I found a bathroom, threw up, and rushed to the side stage so I wouldn't miss my call. I played two songs with Stevie that night, still pretty high, but also naturally exhilarated. A potent mix.

The next day, Doug and I drove south to Calgary and did it all over again at the Jubilee Auditorium, though happily this time without the cocaine. I was in blues heaven, lucky to be there, and I knew it. Stevie had booked his next show for Vancouver at the Commodore, and so after the gig in Calgary, Doug and I hurried back across the mountains to catch him at the iconic venue that's played host to everyone from the Red Hot Chili Peppers to David Bowie to Tina Turner over the years. It was a room made for loud rock 'n' roll, and I wasn't going to miss Stevie there, even if he already had another opener booked. It was special to be in the audience that evening—somehow it made me appreciate the nights I'd watch from the side stage even more.

The show, of course, was incredible, one of those legendary concerts people still talk about in Vancouver. Stevie didn't call me up that night, which was a slight disappointment, but one easily offset by the power of seeing someone so dialed into his instrument that at times he seemed to float above the stage.

We hung out a bit after the show, and Stevie asked if I was interested in flying down to Arizona in a few weeks to see a benefit concert featuring Don Henley, Bonnie Raitt, Jackson Browne, Stevie Nicks, and Stevie himself. This was asked casually, as though the answer could be anything at all, like it wasn't a 100 percent guarantee that I was going to say yes immediately. That was something special about Stevie—a certain casualness, or a lack of presumption, as if he was genuinely curious to know if I'd have any interest at all in attending such a gathering of icons. I wondered aloud how on earth I'd make it to Tucson, and Stevie handed me the card of a woman from his management company named Edi Johnson. "Phone Edi tomorrow and tell her that I want to buy you a ticket to Arizona for the show, okay? She'll know about it by then, and she'll take care of you," he said. Just like that: more magic.

I had some questions. What would I do for money? What would I do after this concert in Tucson? Where was my life, suddenly so energized with possibility and opportunity, ultimately going? But it wasn't time for those things. When opportunity knocks, you don't ask questions. You answer the door.

CHAPTER ELEVEN

AUSTIN-BOUND

AT THE CORNER OF Williams and Commercial Drive in East Vancouver stood an iconic coffee shop named Joe's. If you ever walked Commercial, you might remember the mural on the side of the building that featured a huge cup of coffee being held aloft by an arching rainbow. Joe's was an institution, really, there for almost fifty years until it finally closed its doors in 2024. It was an old-school place, full of grouchy regulars and snooker tables and some pinball machines. I felt right at home there, so much so that I basically used the place as my office during those years in Vancouver. It had everything I needed: good cheap coffee, some diversions for when I was bored, and, crucially, a pay phone. Around that time I'd had some difficulties keeping up with my phone bill at the apartment and the good folks at the utility had seen fit to discontinue my service, so I relied on that line at Joe's to conduct whatever business I had to do.

Relatedly, I also loved the place because Joe, sweetheart that he was, would let me run a tab when resources were scarce. Another place across the street called Santos Tapas, run by Santos himself, did the same. Between the two, I could eat and stay caffeinated when I was broke, and I was deeply grateful for the ways in which my adopted hometown looked out for me. I always made sure to pay them back, and I never forgot their kindness.

So it was to Joe's that I headed the next day when it was time to call Edi Johnson about that flight to Tucson. I was nervous, of course, but I needn't have been. Edi, who was based in Austin, was absolutely lovely. Stevie had told her all about me, and she'd already booked a ticket for one Colin Munn aboard United Airlines, and all I had to do was head to the airport in Vancouver on September 19 for the flight to Arizona. I scribbled the details and flight number on a scrap of paper, thanked her profusely, and floated out of Joe's onto the Drive, once again unable to believe my good fortune. As I settled into the feeling, though, some of those pesky questions started to come back into my mind, the most pressing of which was: How on earth was I going to pay for anything? Stevie picking up the tab for the ticket helped immensely, but I couldn't just count on genius musicians to cover my bills. I had to eat, presumably had to get from place to place, and I'd need somewhere to sleep. I scraped together what little money

I could for a few days before finally accepting reality: There was no way I could make this trip without selling something to get the cash.

Unfortunately, I didn't have much to sell. At the time, I was still playing that Ibanez Artist, and while I wasn't exactly expecting to get called up on stage to join Stevie Ray Vaughan as he perhaps duetted with, I don't know . . . Bonnie Raitt or Don Henley or something, I would need to take that guitar with me so I'd have something to play in whatever circumstances emerged. That left the massive Fender Twin I'd been given by Billy Cowsill as payment for a week of cancelled work and my beloved acoustic that my parents had commissioned Peter Sawchyn to make for me in Regina when I was just a kid. A dilemma for sure, but after some reflection I realized I had no choice but to sell these things. What waited for me in Tucson, I reasoned, could make it all worthwhile, as painful as it was to part with the acoustic in particular.

There was a record store on Commercial, near my apartment, and I spent a lot of time there poring over vinyl and chatting with the clerks, who were nice guys. They had a bulletin board full of homemade ads—bassists looking for bands, bands looking for bassists, somebody offering flute lessons, that kind of thing—and I thought I'd put an ad for my acoustic and amp up there. But before I could even tack it to the board, one of the employees, a guy named Alex, who also wrote for one of the local entertainment papers, said he was interested and asked me how much I was looking for. I thought for a second and blurted out a thousand bucks, a number that seemed very fair to me, the sort of price that should get the gear sold right away.

Alex countered with seven hundred. I took a deep breath, considered my better judgment, decided to go against it, and told him we had a deal. My beautiful, handmade Sawchyn, my constant companion for years, gone, just like that. I'd get it back down the road, but that's a story for another day.

While it wouldn't be quite right to say I was full of regret—I truly felt I had no choice—I was sad about selling my stuff. But, as has been the case so many times in my life, my blue mood was soon lifted by the power of music. Right before I was scheduled to leave Vancouver, a rumour started going around town that Aerosmith and some members of Iron Maiden might make a guest appearance at a local club called Club Soda where a band called the Payolas were playing. The Payolas were a loosely new wave group from Vancouver, co-founded by British-born singer Paul Hyde and Victoria-born producer Bob Rock, both of whom I knew a little bit at the time. Sure enough, after they played their first set, they got Iron Maiden's lead singer Bruce Dickinson up for a song. And then, to my surprise, they got me up on stage to play a slow blues through Bob's guitar rig, with Dickinson on vocals. What a trip that was. Later that night, Aerosmith all got up and played "Walk This Way" and tore the roof off the place. Even later than that, that same Bob Rock would become my first real producer. But I'll come back to that.

It was tough to pack for a trip with a one-way ticket and no real itinerary. How long would I be in Tucson? Would I come back right after the benefit? Might Stevie actually call me up for a song? Hard to know, but I couldn't stop thinking about it all. My dad had recently relocated to Vancouver and found an apartment in the same building as me, so when the day of my departure arrived, he was happy to borrow somebody's car and drive me to the airport. I had my luggage, containing my best guess at what I'd need for this mystery trip, my seven hundred dollars, and my sunburst Ibanez. We set off into destiny.

But destiny had different ideas, or at least the customs officer did. Check-in was fine, but by the time I got up to the little pre-clearance counter, things got complicated.

"What's your destination?" said the unsmiling man behind the glass, a square-headed, crew-cutted older guy.

"I've been invited to Tucson, Arizona, by my favourite guitarist, Stevie Ray Vaughan! Jackson Browne and Stevie Nicks and Tom Petty and all kinds of other artists will be there. He bought me this ticket! And maybe I'll be able to sit in for a couple of songs!"

I enthusiastically shared all this, assuming this stoic fellow would be as excited as I was at this news.

"Let me see your ID," he said unenthusiastically.

I fished my social insurance card and frayed birth certificate out of a plastic sheath and handed them over.

"No credit card on you?" he asked.

"Credit card? I don't have any credit card," I said. "But I do have seven hundred dollars!"

I was starting to think this wasn't going very well.

"I see you've got a guitar with you there," he said. "You mentioned playing some songs. So you'll be working down there, I take it?"

"Well, no, I mean, not really working . . . I hope to get to sit in with my hero. Maybe I'll meet some people in the business. But it's not like a job!"

There was a long pause as he looked deep into my hopes and dreams. He didn't like what he saw.

"You're not going anywhere, son," he said. "Come back when you have the proper paperwork and a work permit."

I was devastated. I stood there, stunned, and then tried one more time.

"But Stevie bought this ticket. He's expecting me. What am I going to do now?"

"Not my problem," he said. And then, looking to the person behind me in line, he barked, "Next!"

Totally deflated, I phoned my roommate Doug, told him what had happened, and waited for him to kindly pick me up so I could start to figure out a plan to save this terrible situation. A scheme did emerge, and in desperation I went back down to my office at Joe's Café to use the pay phone to call my uncle Doug. If I could talk him into driving me across the border, I could get a flight from Seattle. Thankfully, Uncle Doug was up for it, and said that we could stay at my grandparents' house the next night. The only problem with this plan was that I'd miss the show in Tucson, which was set for that very night. So my next call was to Edi Johnson, to whom I explained the whole border debacle before asking, sheepishly, if there was some way I could still come down from Seattle. Edi told me she'd need to talk to Stevie, and to hold tight and ring her back in a few hours. I waited, sitting in a mix of anticipation and embarrassment, wondering what Stevie would think of my border-crossing incompetence. Would he even want me to come down, now that the Tucson gig was going to be missed?

When I phoned Edi back a while later, she'd spoken to Stevie and it was all good. He would fly me from Seattle to Austin, get me a room at a motel, and I could hang out there and meet some of his friends at the legendary Antone's, Austin's home of the blues. Once again in disbelief at my good fortune, I went home to get ready.

Uncle Doug picked me up and miraculously we cruised across the border as we headed to Seattle to stay with Grandma Kay and Grandpa Joe, who enjoyed hearing about my ongoing saga. Or at least Grandma Kay did. Grandpa Joe's surliness was still his defining feature, so it was hard to tell if he ever enjoyed anything. That night, lying in a bed Grandma Kay made up for me on the sofa, my mind wandered far and wide, excited about what was to come, and full of dreams about what might happen. I was so excited I couldn't sleep, but even if I hadn't been, I'd have struggled to rest because of the plethora of clocks they kept in the house. You could hear them all ticking away, out of sync with each other. And then the hour would come, usually just as I was finally drifting off, and the first clock would ring its low *dong . . . dong . . .* sound, only to be followed by many more. Some of them even chimed at the half or quarter hours. It was basically torture, and I was thrilled when the morning light finally started to fill the sky.

In Austin, I hopped into a cab and headed to the Stars Motel, the place Edi had booked for me. It was a seedy little spot, underneath an overpass if memory serves me correctly, and as I walked to my room after checking in, I noticed a beer bottle floating in the outdoor pool—a classy touch. I was too hyped to stay in my room and watch TV on my first night in Texas, and it was early enough in the evening to try to catch a show, so I made my way to the legendary Antone's, where I was astonished to find the Fabulous Thunderbirds playing that very night. What luck! I listened to them all the time then and played a lot of songs off their albums in my own repertoire. That night I met Clifford Antone, the owner of Antone's, and a few people from the local scene, including Kim Wilson and the T-Birds as well as local guitar legend Denny Freeman and sax player Kaz Kazanoff, among others. It kind of felt like I was suddenly walking among giants, even if Stevie himself wasn't around.

Those days in Austin were a bit of a blur, catching as much music as I could, soaking it all up. Unexpectedly, the most memorable thing that happened had nothing to do with the amazing events all around me, but rather a phone call from back in Vancouver. Somehow, Steve Macklam, the Vancouver-based manager whom Larry Wanagas had told me he was teaming up with over lunch at the Palliser Hotel, tracked me down in Austin and rang me up to say he'd like to represent me. I was pretty thrilled to get this call. We chatted and hit it off. I told Steve about what I was seeing in Austin, and how things had been going generally for me. He told me to contact him as soon as I got back to Vancouver, and I promised I would.

I had a lovely day with my telephone friend Edi Johnson, who picked me up at the motel and showed me around the city. She even took me out to the racetrack owned by Stevie's manager, her employer, Chelsey Milliken. Edi was kind and attentive, and in addition to touring me around, she wanted to know how I was doing. I decided to be honest: I was having a lot of fun, but I was going to run out of money pretty soon, and I didn't know what I was going to do. She must have tracked Stevie down on the road shortly after that and told him about my predicament, because later she phoned me at the motel and said that he had offered to buy me a plane ticket to Cleveland, where he'd be playing the next day. I was relieved and grateful as I packed up to continue this trip of a lifetime.

In Cleveland, I arrived at the hotel where Stevie and the band were staying—I knew I was in the right place because their tour bus was parked right out front. I ran into the road manager and some of the crew in the lobby, said hello, then checked into the room that was waiting for me. Later, I made my way back down to the lobby, guitar case in hand, where Stevie and the band were milling about for bus call and the ride to the venue for sound check. Stevie warmly welcomed me, ever gracious, and I was glad for the chance to thank him personally for the incredible generosity he was showing me. I was nervous and excited to see him, as always, and hoped he would be happy to see me after all this trouble he had gone to to make this happen.

The band was booked in a venue where Elvis Costello had played the night before—it was 1985 and he was big—and I stood with my typical huge grin on my face, watching them sound check from side stage. They were on fire, as usual, even without an audience. Since I'd seen them last, they'd added Reese Wynans on keys and had a fuller sound. Plus they had three records under their belt by then—*Texas Flood*, *Couldn't Stand the Weather*, and *Soul to Soul*—so they had so much material to choose from, in addition to Stevie's command of so many reimagined blues standards. Every night I watched them play, I'd always be waiting to hear "Change It," as I loved the chord progression on that song so much. Plus, who doesn't enjoy a raunchy Texas shuffle? Later that night, as the show wound down, that familiar anxious feeling appeared in the pit of my stomach. Would I be called up to play with them? What song would it be? Is this actually happening? Sure enough, after the first encore, Stevie approached the mic and said, "Ladies and gentlemen, please welcome to the stage a friend of ours from Vancouver, Canada, Colin Munn." It was happening again!

The next show on the schedule was in Ann Arbor, Michigan, which meant I was about to be treated to my first ever extended ride on a real touring bus. I felt a little funny being in the band's space, so I tried to keep cool and stay out of their way as much as possible. But it was hard to stay cool when I was living a dream, and hard to stay out of the way in the cramped quarters of the bus. When we got to Ann Arbor, I made my way to the front, where Stevie was sleeping on one of the couches in the lounge. I peeked out the window and saw fans everywhere. Some were holding signs that said things like I LOVE YOU STEVIE! More than a few were even dressed like him, skulking around, hoping to catch a glimpse of their hero. But I didn't need to skulk, because I was on the bus, and he was right in front of me. Most of the crew and the band had headed inside the Michigan Theater to set up, so I just sat down and allowed myself to take it all in. I looked across the bus at the sleeping Stevie. Eventually, I found myself focusing on his big hands, resting on his chest as he snoozed. I stared at them and thought, "Those are the hands that create all this magic." Truly a surreal moment.

That night, I once again waited side stage to see if I'd get the call. I always tried to stand near René Martinez's guitar stand—visible, but without being too obvious about it, and without crowding René. After the main set Stevie came over to talk to his tech for a minute, and then came over to me.

"Hey, I'm going to call you up after a couple of songs, okay?" he said.

"That would be amazing, Stevie. Thank you!"

"Hey, do you want me to call you Colin Munn? Or Colin James?"

I had told Stevie that my name was sometimes a problem. People always got it wrong—Colin Mutt, Colin Mud, Colin Mund . . . I'd heard them all. I'd even got in the habit of spelling it as soon as I said it, just to get ahead of things. I had talked to him about maybe using my middle name, James, as my stage name to save everyone the confusion.

"Colin James," I shouted over the crowd screaming for the encore.

And thus it was that on the night of September 27, 1985, I became Colin James, Stevie being the first person to utter my new stage name.

"I hope you don't mind," Stevie said a bit later, stepping to the mic, "but we're gonna have some fun. Ladies and gentlemen, from Austin, Texas, via Vancouver, Canada . . . Colin James!"

We played a few numbers, and Stevie even got me to sing a Magic Sam song called "You Belong to Me," giving me something extra to do, as though he knew this night would end up being a pivotal moment in my life. Later that night, the soundman was nice enough to hand me a cassette of the point in the show when I joined the band during the encore. I still have it to this day, though I can't listen to it—my voice is so shallow and throaty. I hadn't really learned how to sing yet.

We carried on down the road on the tour, and for the next few nights Stevie would generally try to get me on stage, but not always. When he didn't, I'd be disappointed, but I always understood. You can't always get what you want, and I was getting it most of the time—but, a guy could get used to this! But all good things come to an end and, unfortunately, my time on the road with Stevie was no exception. And I'm sorry to say that it was my fault that it ended.

We had a night off somewhere in Chicago and a bunch of people from the tour were hanging around in the back lounge of the bus. I was just mingling and generally enjoying myself when I noticed that people were passing around a little cylindrical thing that looked a bit like a pepper mill. I deduced that it must be a kind of cocaine grinder. Like I said, I'd done a bit of cocaine before, a line here or there at a party, and of course that epic line that Stevie had prepared backstage in Edmonton. But I'd never seen anything quite like this—it collected the fine powder in a little well that was quite deep. When it made its way around me, I nervously took the rolled-up dollar bill and tried to select just a little bit of coke off the corner of the big pile in the well. I had no idea what I was doing, and in a split second the whole pile had gone straight up my nose. Time stood still as the drugs hit my brain, and in horror I slowly realized what I'd done. I wasn't the only one horrified. As I looked around this motley crew, I watched them all one by one realize what had happened, and they were *not* happy about it.

"I'm sorry," I yelped. "I didn't mean to do that! I'm so sorry!"

"You can't bullshit a bullshitter, man," someone growled from down the way.

"No, honestly!" I declared earnestly. "I would never do that on purpose. I'm so sorry, guys!"

The mood got super dark, super fast, one of those moments where you realize you just may have made enemies out of everyone sitting around you. My heart was pounding with nerves and drugs, and I felt as terrible as I did high, which was to say *very*. I got my key at the front desk and did the walk of shame back to my room, the existential dread growing in me with each step. When I got there, I lay on my bed freaking out. I had ruined everything, and I was so high I felt as if I could barely hold on to reality. I phoned a few friends back home to fess up, then lay awake in bed for hours, staring at the ceiling, feeling awful, before falling into a shallow, teeth-chattering sleep.

The next morning, there was a knock at my door. I opened it, and there to my utter shock was Stevie himself. I looked at him imploringly and stammered something about how I hadn't meant to do anything wrong and how sorry I was. He looked at me for a bit and then, to my surprise and relief, grabbed me in a long, heartfelt embrace, holding me close.

"You shouldn't be around all that, it's wrong, and I'm really sorry that all happened. It will be okay," he said, and then left.

When I think about that moment now, it really shows what a thoughtful man he was. To come to my room in person like that, to give me so much along the way—these things were truly extraordinary. And of course it wasn't just me, he'd shone a light on so many other artists, like Canada's Jeff Healey, David Gogo, Ronnie Baker Brooks, Bernard Allison, and I'm sure many, many others. We were all lifted up and guided by his genius and unbelievable natural talent. Stevie would later confront his addictions after suffering a complete collapse in Europe, and he would spend the rest of his too-short life sober. The time I had with him was precious, and I am grateful for each and every moment our paths crossed. We'd meet up a few more times down the road, but those are stories for another day.

A little while later, Stevie's tour manager phoned to say they'd booked me on a flight back to Vancouver. Was I devastated? Absolutely. Was I a little relieved? Definitely. This was all so much, perhaps almost too much, at least for me, right then. It was time to go home. I was twenty-one years old, and it was time to start my own band.

CHAPTER TWELVE

A BAND OF MY OWN

MY NEW MANAGER Steve Macklam lived in a house on Laurel Street, near Cambie in the Fairview area of Vancouver. It was a cool neighbourhood full of older homes and it had a nice, genteel vibe. Steve's place was a one-storey Arts and Crafts house typical of the area at the time. When I returned to town after the debacle in Chicago, I started hanging around at Steve's a lot. We quickly became fast friends, as I did with his wife, Caroline Luxford, who had a thick cockney accent straight out of London's East End. Their place was full of books about the music business and salacious Hollywood tragedies. Steve had a special interest in Elvis's early years, so much so that they had named their big English setter Elvis. Steve, Elvis, and I would pass the time sitting around the house talking, planning, and listening to records.

Steve and Caroline had been instrumental in Vancouver's burgeoning punk scene in the late seventies and early eighties, and Steve had a reputation for spotting talent and pairing that talent with the right record label. He was also well-read, with an English degree and a background in journalism. He could relate well to musicians but was also comfortable with record company executives and A. & R. (artists and repertoire) people, using that university degree to spin impressive yarns about his clients. He was very good with both sides of that equation. The further removed I became from my Stevie Ray Vaughan American Blues Odyssey, the more surreal the whole music business seemed, as though it was a hallucination, or some intense dream I would soon snap out of. As I came back down to earth, Steve and Caroline's place became a kind of home base for me where I regrouped and started to plan for the future.

I knew I needed to form a band, but before I could do that, I needed to decide what kind of music I wanted to play. This might seem backwards, but this was going to be *my* band, and so I needed to figure out *my* vision and then find the players to fit that vision. Happily, that was a joyful process that grew naturally out of hanging out with like-minded musicians around the scene and listening to records with Steve. We'd sit around spinning albums and debating songs, thinking out loud about what might fit on a future set list for my theoretical band. We made notes, we made lists, and we thought about how various songs would create a balanced, blues-forward musical style.

As Steve and I worked, a many-faceted picture started to emerge. We had blues, of course, but also jump blues—a boisterous, energetic, horn-laden rhythm and blues that heralded the birth of rock 'n' roll—and naturally a few powerful ballads. We were looking to artists both new and old, like Los Lobos, Albert King, the Blasters, Junior Wells, the Neville Brothers, and Robert Cray, to name a few, for inspiration. We'd hit the straight blues, as you'd expect, and tuck in some Chester Burnett and McKinley Morganfield (perhaps better known as Howlin' Wolf and Muddy Waters), but we'd also play more obscure songs from artists like Jackie Wilson, Rosco Gordon, and Roy Brown. A lot of the material we explored then would eventually lead me to the music we would cut for the Little Big Band many years later. There was one song that was a real standout, a slow blues called "Why'd You Lie" on a record that Steve had in his collection. It was written by a relatively unknown songwriter from Detroit, now living in Canada, by the name of Morgan Davis. It really grabbed both of us, and we put it on the list as a great choice for a cover.

Once I felt confident in the music we'd be making, it was time to gather the players. I started playing with local guys, people I already knew and had played with, trying to find that elusive chemistry that makes a band work. I had a firm grasp of the mysterious power that makes some musicians gel and some fail to click. I'd put years into the Hoodoo Men, David Burgin and the Nightshades, and, most recently, Billy Cowsill's Trainwreck, and I had seen all varieties of musical chemistry—some of it sublime and surprising, some of it downright disastrous. It's hard to explain what makes a band work, but you know it when you feel it, and so I set out to feel my way through all the options I could.

First I hired a local drummer, a guy named Andy Graffiti, who played in a few popular roots-type bands. Andy had a little low-rise rehearsal space in a dubious part of town right across from a strip club called the No5 Orange, known locally as "The Five." Andy was a thoughtful drummer who could play in a variety of styles, and, I admit, his rehearsal space was a bonus. At first I had my old friend Roger Brant, whom I'd first known as a member of Houndog and whom I'd played with in the Nightshades, come on board to play bass. Roger was the perfect person to start with because he knew a lot of classic blues material and also had a biting and dark sense of humour that I enjoyed. I wanted a Hammond organ player, which felt crucial to the sound I was chasing, and I had in mind a guy I had seen in Alberta named Rick Hopkins. Rick was a natural player who also happened to be very funny, and gifted with an uncanny knack for completing crossword puzzles at astonishing speed. In Calgary, while playing with Billy Cowsill, I had seen Rick play in a trio with another drummer named Darrell Mayes, whom I was interested in as well. They were a killer duo when they played behind a talented songwriter and guitar player by the name of Gaye Delorme. Gaye was famous for a hit novelty song called "The Rodeo Song" that had the memorable line "Well it's 40 below and I don't give a fuck, Got a heater in my truck and I'm off to the rodeo."

Andy was great to help get us off the ground, but I thought that Darrell, a lefty drummer with an imposing build and hard-hitting style that I found very compelling, would be a perfect fit. I reached out to Rick to ask if he and Darrell would consider coming out to Vancouver to see if things clicked. Rick and his girlfriend had just had a baby, so the timing was tricky, but in the end the two players made their way out for a rehearsal in Vancouver. We found places for them to stay while in town, crashing on friends' couches, and I hopefully and impatiently awaited the first rehearsal. Just as I had imagined it would, the rehearsal went great, and even without a bass player the band sounded pretty full. Rick would sometimes use the floor pedals on the Hammond for bass when playing with Gaye Delorme's three-piece, so that helped fill out the sound a lot. Once we found the right bass player—Roger was great, but we'd decided to go in a different direction—we would be killing it for sure.

The busy and in-demand Andy Graffiti was kind enough to let us use his seedy but useful space for these early rehearsals, and we quickly gelled and began to arrange for Rick and Darrell to move to Vancouver permanently so we could get things going. At some point, someone told me about a local Capilano jazz school bass player named Mark Weston, who auditioned with us. He and drummer Darrell sounded great together, so he ended up taking the bass chair going forward.

Once the lineup was set, we started playing in earnest as the Colin James Band in clubs around Vancouver—we debuted at the Savoy in May 1986—and out of town whenever and wherever we could. One of our earliest test shows as a touring band was a trip out to my old stomping grounds to play the Regina Folk Festival that summer. Steve was nervous about how my newly formed band would manage on our own, but we came home sporting a rave review in the *Leader-Post* newspaper along with a new-found confidence in our nascent band. Once Steve read the review, I dare say he had some added confidence as well.

Soon enough those gigs were generating a bit of local buzz, and in October of the same year we were booked on a triple bill playing the famous Commodore Ballroom, where I'd seen Stevie himself play earlier in the year. The show was a benefit for the New Democratic Party, featuring me and the band, the newly founded and Celtic-inspired Spirit of the West, and the quickly ascending cowpunk star k.d. lang. I was psyched to be on this bill, and to be playing that venue in particular. But also a little bit daunted. k.d. was known for her intense and theatrical stage show, and when Steve and I started planning my set, we knew we'd have to do something special to grab some attention on the big night. We zeroed in on a Roy Brown song called "Hard Luck Blues." You might not know it, but you definitely know "Heartbreak Hotel," Elvis's first number one hit, which was said to remind the King of Roy Brown's song when he first heard the lyrics. "Hard Luck Blues" is incredible, opening with an unforgettable first few lines: "Well, rocks is my pillow, the cold ground is my bed, the highway is my home, so I might as well be dead." We took our inspiration from these words, and the night of the show I ended up singing next to a stage set featuring a large tombstone made of spray-painted Styrofoam with *RIP* written in big letters across it. Pretty tacky! But it seemed to work well enough on the night itself, which turned out to be a real success. I'd go on to play that room again and again in the years to come, so my tombstone blues that night were the start of a special relationship.

By late 1986, we were ready to start properly touring, which is how we'd spend much of the next few years—criss-crossing the country, building a following one show at a time. In those days, a band would often play a whole week in the same club, Monday to Saturday, which was great because it gave you some time to build an audience as the week went on. You might have a light house on Monday, but if you did your job right, the audience would grow as buzz and word of mouth took over Halifax or Kingston or whatever town you were in. By the weekend, if all went well, you'd have a packed room, often full of many repeat customers. The first time we played the legendary Horseshoe Tavern in Toronto, we had a thin crowd on Monday, even though we were riding some hype at the time. But by Saturday night the lineup to get into the club ran down the street. Progress like that, in turn, meant you'd get hired again, when you crossed back across the country, and it also meant that most likely your next Monday night would be fuller than the last. Lather, rinse, repeat, all the way across Canada and back, over and over again. Nowadays, such runs are unheard of, which is too bad; I'd have to imagine that social media would have made that buzz grow even louder as a week went on, but back then there was none of that, of course. It was word of mouth and old-school press—radio, TV, and newspapers. That was it!

I remember one time in these early days, I was acting as band leader and road manager for a small run of shows. I had been paid around three thousand dollars that night and I had tucked the envelope of cash in my ridiculously heavy briefcase and checked us into the hotel. We all got our room keys and traipsed through the lobby towards the elevator, and when it arrived, I quickly set the briefcase and one bag inside the elevator and turned to get another when . . . to my horror, the elevator and all the money and bags went up ten floors. I seriously panicked and thought the worst might come of it. But happily, everything was found, and I learned a valuable lesson: Get a road manager to do that kind of thing from now on! Live and learn.

We made these road trips in an ugly maroon-and-silver Econoline van that had previously belonged to a band that had been managed by Larry Wanagas. We practically lived in that damned van the whole time, driving across the endless expanse of Canada again and again, often stupefied by boredom. We'd pass the time with inane jokes and the occasional bout of day drinking. Countless times we'd pull up to a hotel and open our sliding door only to have bottles and cans and various detritus fall out, embarrassingly. Anybody passing by would probably have had little doubt what we did for a living. That van went back and forth across the country many, many times before we decided to sell it after the repair bill was too high following a particular service call. I loved every one of those trips. I was doing what my heroes did: playing music every night, trying to thrill an audience, building a fan base. It was an exhausting kind of heaven, and I adored it. I also adored driving that van a touch too fast;

I would use it recreationally when I returned home from touring and received so many speeding tickets that one day I got a letter in the mail saying my licence would be revoked if I got another!

On our way back to Vancouver from one of these trips, we stopped in Winnipeg and played a show to a full house. The next day, we had a day off, so I had a very welcome chance to catch up with some old friends, many of whom I hadn't seen since I lived there some years before. I also ran into my ex-girlfriend and fellow Quaker, Sunshine Ackerman. I was thrilled to run into Sunny—it had been too long, and so much had changed for us both. She now had a boyfriend whom I knew a bit from when I lived in town, and they had a brand new baby daughter. It was wonderful to see her so happy. I think Sunny felt the same way about me, glad to know that my move to Vancouver had worked out. We reminisced about some old times, and I remember looking at her baby girl and thinking, "Wow, that could have been us . . ."

When I got back to Vancouver, exhausted from the road, I took my acoustic guitar and a half mickey of vodka to the little park on Commercial Drive, right across from my "office" at Joe's Café. It was a lazy afternoon, and I was just hanging out, passing the time, decompressing, when a song came to me. I hadn't written a lot of my own songs at that time, and I was surprised to find this one just sort of writing itself. Later, I'd learn that songs often arrive like that, out of thin air, but that day it was a fresh feeling, and I chased it down. The song was in the key of B, and originally it had a slight rolling, country feel to it. It started with the words "Girl I see ya, holding hands with your lover and you're making plans with each other and it looks real good on you. Don't you worry, I didn't come to make things strange, 'cause there's a reason that things change, there's nothing we can do." That was it, totally natural. When it came time to find the chorus, it came naturally too, drawn straight from my own life experience: "It's been five long years . . . " It was spilling out of me, emerging from the epiphany I'd had in Winnipeg a few days before, and it felt great to get it down. Paths not taken, simple twists of fate . . . I finished most of it right there in the park, little bottle of vodka by my side, and hurried home to play it for my roommate before calling Steve to tell him all about it.

CHAPTER THIRTEEN

SIGNED, SEALED, DELIVERED

THE SONG I'D WRITTEN in the little park in East Van was well-received by everybody in our circle, and Steve figured that between "Five Long Years" and the Morgan Davis song "Why'd You Lie," I had the material to do some actual recording. We'd previously cut a few demos in a tiny studio at the back of the management office, called Snug Studios, which was run by Willie MacCalder, the piano player for the Powder Blues Band who had given me advice at Mama Gold's about not having to wait around the back of the room to get into this scene, that I should just come walking in right through the front door. But those were just rough takes that we'd send to club owners so they could get an idea of our sound and what to expect from booking us. Now Steve thought I was ready to move to a proper studio. And he had an idea about who could help us do that, a hotshot young Vancouver producer named Bob Rock—who also played in the band the Payolas.

Steve knew Bob through a record Bob had produced for the Pointed Sticks, who at the time were a successful Vancouver new wave band managed by Steve. They'd garnered a strong local following, and signed with Stiff Records in the UK after being passed on by Seymour Stein at Reprise in the US. Bob agreed to work with us on a two-song EP, and we set a date at Vancouver's Little Mountain Sound Studios, which was Bob's home base. I talked to Bob on the phone so we could get to know each other a bit before the session and he told me he really liked "Five Long Years." He'd started his career at Little Mountain as a recording engineer and then became a producer, and he was one of the main reasons so many huge eighties acts made the pilgrimage to the studio. Aerosmith, Bon Jovi, Mötley Crüe, and Metallica all recorded there, and Little Mountain became famous for a particular drum sound they got by recording snare drums in the loading bay where they could capture the unique natural reverb.

In addition to our rough demos with Willie, I'd done a little recording a few years earlier in Saskatchewan, and I'd self-engineered a couple of amateur things on a Tascam four-track—I taped "Three Hours Past Midnight" at a buddy's house once—but Little Mountain was a whole new ball game. It was the mid-eighties now, and our first day in a "real" studio like Little Mountain was unbelievable for me and the guys in the band. The massive Studer reel-to-reel two-inch tape machines and the warm red lights of the vintage gear in the racks, the swarms of cables in the patchbay and the mesmerizing SSL console with the little video readout—all too much, and just perfectly perfect. I liked this a lot!

We tackled “Why’d You Lie” first, and the bed track, including that long guitar intro, was finished pretty quickly, in two takes. I played the only Strat I had at the time, which was a Fender Squire. It may have been the only guitar of mine to make the record, because for “Five Long Years” I played one of Bob’s Telecasters through a Hiwatt, a British amp that’s probably most commonly associated with David Gilmour and the Who; they’re known for their clean headroom and they can get *really* loud. Bob suggested we create an instrumental chord progression to use as a bridge with a guitar solo and an added harmony, and voilà! The song was done. Both tracks were completed in a couple of days. Hearing the mix for the first time, sitting in Little Mountain when Bob put the big speakers on full blast, was totally exhilarating. As we waited around for the album artwork to be completed, and then for the vinyl to be pressed, I felt we’d recorded something really special. How it would be received, I couldn’t say. But I was super proud of what we’d done.

In those pre-streaming days, radio was king and stations had a fair amount of latitude to play what they pleased; playlists were less regimented, perhaps especially on rock radio. We were all a little concerned that the almost minute-long solo that begins “Why’d You Lie” might be cut—or, worse, talked over by the DJ! At the time, a lot of people would release radio edits of songs, with things like instrumentals and solos cut down to make the tracks shorter and more friendly for airplay. But I didn't want to do that—that intro was essential to the mood of my interpretation of Davis's song. Without it, the song would be just a standard cover, but with it, I'd given it my personal stamp, and I felt that's what made it work.

At the time, I was staying in the Europe Hotel in Gastown, in low-income housing, and I was living hand to mouth, day to day, getting by on what we earned on gigs but without any real stability. But that EP was the start of something, and I didn't even need to look at the airplay reports to know that. One day I walked into a convenience store to buy cigarettes and I heard something that sounded familiar. It took me a few seconds to realize it was my own song playing on the radio. In fact, I was hearing the very intro I'd been so worried would get cut by stations. I laughed as I listened incredulously—we had *just* recorded that song, and here it was, piped through the speakers in the corner store. I walked up to the counter, asked for my smokes, and couldn't resist saying to the clerk, "That's my song! That's me!" He looked at me, unmoved, and said, "Good for you, buddy." After that, I started hearing the songs everywhere around town, on the radio in bars, coming out of the windows of passing cars. They were picking up steam, and I was delighted by that, at least when I happened to hear them.

My music began to travel, too, as we mailed copies of the EP to stations across the country, and even hand-delivered one to KXRX in Seattle, and they started playing both songs on heavy rotation.

Airplay increased to the point that in 1987 I was even nominated for my first award, courtesy of Toronto radio station CFNY—a CASBY award for Most Promising Artist. Something was happening, and you could feel it. And it felt *good*.

For a long time, we'd played in Vancouver almost exclusively at the Savoy, an amazing club across the street from the hotel where I was living. It was on the second floor, held maybe two hundred people, and was a great, intimate place to play. As things picked up with radio airplay, we moved to the slightly larger Town Pump, also in Gastown, a bit bigger, with more standing room. I loved playing the smaller clubs where you could slowly start to connect with an audience in a completely intimate way, until you're all just one rocking entity, having fun and feeding off each other's energy. That is seriously addictive stuff and something I still love about playing live today.

It was an exciting time to be on the scene in Vancouver. Expo 86 was bringing the world to our doorstep, so local musicians had a lot of work, and a bunch of major acts were booked around that time to capitalize on the excitement. Stevie came through town with Bonnie Raitt on a double bill, and I had the pleasure of meeting her for the first time backstage, which would be the start of a long friendship. To this day I love Bonnie, for so many reasons. Of course, I admire her social justice and human rights advocacy. And it goes without saying I think she's an incredible player and singer. But I also just love the way she treats her fans and guests; after a Bonnie show, she makes time to have a few words with absolutely every person invited backstage.

Steve was doing his thing, too, talking to labels far and wide about me, ginning up some excitement. Around 1987, there were whispers about an A. & R. woman at A&M Records in Los Angeles who was especially interested in us, asking Steve a lot of questions about me. But he had a lot of irons in the fire, and I tried not to get too distracted by the business side of things, just letting him do what he did best—hype little old me! Steve was great at that, and soon enough word came down that a woman named Nancy Jeffries was going to fly up from LA with a few other execs to see a show I had coming up at the Town Pump. Naturally, this made me very nervous. But just as naturally, it made me very determined to play it super cool. All of us tried our best to seem like we really didn't care. If they liked it, sure, yeah, that's nice. If they didn't, that's fine, no problem, they just didn't get it, wouldn't have been right for us anyway.

When the day finally came, I struggled to keep that cool, and was overwhelmed with butterflies in my stomach. But I also had an idea, and I found out what table the execs would be at so that I could make good on it.

That night, we rocked the place, and about three-quarters of the way through our set I knew the time had come. The LA folks were sitting off on stage left, just in front of the stage—close, in other words. Close enough that I could jump right onto their table. Would it be too forward? Or would they appreciate the blatant showboating? In the moment it felt right, and so I did it—I jumped off the stage and landed right in the middle of their table, rocking out on a solo, spilling their drinks all over the place. I had no idea if my gamble had paid off—if it made an impression or just annoyed them. But a few days later the call came down. It was Steve, and he wanted to know if I was sitting down . . .

They'd loved it, and I couldn't believe this was actually happening. Steve said the label would have an offer to me in a few days, and it would be coming from the brand new American outpost of the UK's Virgin Records. Virgin had been founded by, among others, Richard Branson, though this was before all the car racing and hot-air balloon stuff. Virgin had had real success with acts like the Sex Pistols and had an association with a lot of prog rock, having scored a massive hit with Mike Oldfield's "Tubular Bells." Now they were expanding into America, and their first few signings included Iggy Pop and Keith Richards—not bad company to be in, I thought to myself!

Steve and I booked flights to LA to meet with Nancy and the team at Virgin Records America, including co-chairmen Jordan Harris and Jeff Ayeroff. Jordan had had a lot to do with Bryan Adams's big successes at A&M Records, and so I was thrilled to meet him. Nancy had been with A&M too—it turned out she'd been the A. & R. woman from A&M who had been asking lots of questions, but she had waited until she moved to Virgin to try to sign me, which is why everything was all of a sudden happening very quickly. We met them all at the tiny headquarters of the new company in a little building on Alden

Drive in Beverly Hills. Afterward, they took us to lunch at the Ivy, which had only been open for a few years but already had its reputation as a see-and-be-seen celebrity hot spot. It was the perfect spot to take a prairie boy to lunch; I was so blown away by the place and everybody in it. It was one of many moments in my life when I felt disbelief at my good fortune, and when I was acutely aware of just how far I'd come from bashing around on my brother's left-handed acoustic guitar in our Regina living room. I looked around the room and saw Julie Andrews. I looked some more and realized that Robert De Niro was sitting two tables away.

Talk soon turned to making my first record. Nancy was a musician herself—she'd been the lead singer in a band called the Insect Trust in the late sixties and early seventies—so she approached the question not just as a seasoned record executive but as someone who could intimately understand the delicacy of these questions for the artist. When would we record? Where would we record? And, perhaps most critically, *who* would produce the thing? Nancy had names in mind, and started listing them. We debated some of them back and forth, pros and cons, talking about records and various possibilities that we liked or disliked. Pretty quickly, one name started to get traction: a man from Miami named Tom Dowd.

CHAPTER FOURTEEN

HERE WE GO

I DON'T THINK I'D ever heard the name Tom Dowd, but I quickly enough learned about his legendary work. He'd spent a long time at Atlantic Records, and engineered and produced everybody—Ray Charles, Diana Ross, Eric Clapton, Ornette Coleman, Aretha Franklin, even John Coltrane. In other words, he'd done it all, and that sounded pretty impressive to me. I would even come to learn that, as a young would-be physicist, he'd worked on the Manhattan Project, helping develop the atomic bomb, even observing the explosions on Bikini Atoll in 1946. How did *that* happen? If we went with Tom, I was told, it would mean recording at Criteria Studios in Miami, his home base.

He recorded so many records there for Atlantic in the seventies that people called it "Atlantic Studio South." In fact, Atlantic Records head Jerry Wexler even kept a session band at the ready there, called the Flyers. James Brown had cut "I Got You (I Feel Good)" in that studio in 1965, and it had gone on to host recording sessions for countless classic artists: Fleetwood Mac, the Eagles, AC/DC, Bob Seger. In the late seventies it was basically home base for the Bee Gees. So while Miami seemed very far away from Vancouver, the thought of working in the same rooms that had given birth to so much amazing music was irresistible.

Before anything formal was set, it was decided that Tom would fly to Toronto to see me play, in July 1987. I had a gig at Harbourfront, opening for the great Albert King, a hero of mine, and it would be the perfect place for Tom to see us live and get a sense of our sound and approach. Tom and I had dinner before the show, talking music and getting to know each other a bit. He mentioned working with another artist who lived in Canada, a guy from Arkansas who'd relocated, and it was none other than Ronnie "The Hawk" Hawkins. I thought to myself that this was the sort of company I would be proud to keep, and I started to get excited about the prospect of what Tom and I could do together. Maybe, one day, I'd be someone he'd be telling stories about to some industry newcomer! The show itself was great, and I had the chance to take some photos with Albert backstage. There's an especially memorable one that always makes me laugh: I am gazing up fondly at this living legend as he smiles for the camera, stylish suspenders and Rolex in place, holding a pipe in one hand and a glass of whisky in the other. It's a perfect photo, or it would be if it weren't for my shirt, which is an atrocity featuring some sort of faux cowhide across its upper chest. That's the eighties for you! Not an especially kind decade for fashion. I think everybody who came up in that era has some regrets, musically and sartorially.

Tom accompanied us back to Vancouver so he could have the chance to meet everybody. We went straight to the headquarters of our little world, the humble address of 1616 West 3rd Street, home to Bumstead Records and Homestead Management, where Larry Wanagas and my manager Steve Macklam worked out of an unassuming second-floor office space. We planned to play Tom some of the demos we'd recorded previously in Snug Studios, the little studio in the back of that same spot. It was so small that you had to go outside to change your mind. Tom listened to our songs and regaled us with unbelievable stories about working with Ron Wood or Rod Stewart or Bobby Darin. Tom and I seemed to click, for the most part, and the stories were certainly alluring. We decided to go with him to produce the record, and we made plans to start recording in December in Miami, just in time to get out of the worst of Vancouver's rainy days.

I called my old buddy Nathan Wiens, who was still living in Regina and now making metal road cases for musicians and bands, and I asked him to make me a few. As we got talking, I realized how much I missed him, and I said that he should move out to Vancouver and join me. Maybe he could come down to Miami and help us with gear, or even come on the road with us to work with the band. My timing was right. Nathan was ready for a change, and he did exactly that. By the time we got to Miami, he was officially working with us, and we ended up rooming together in a cool little art deco hotel in the early days of the South Beach restoration. I was about to record my first album, sun filling the skies, my best friend by my side. Everything was perfect. Or so I thought.

The relationship between artist and producer is a complex one, and it can be very complicated. Usually you can work through whatever challenges arise and find a way to get the job done in a manner that satisfies both parties. In a sense, a producer is the mediator between your art and the record company's more financially driven wishes, so it's important that you're on the same page, or close enough to get there in the end. I wish I could tell you that Tom Dowd and I were on the same page, but it became clear quite quickly that we were not. Tom's stories were amazing, and I'd been seduced by the glamour and romance of them. And his track record was undeniable.

In retrospect, I think part of the reason he was so successful for so long was his ability to move with the times, to follow the trends, and to help artists connect to the sounds of the moment. But sounds of the moment don't necessarily mix with old, storied styles of music, styles like the blues, and we found ourselves in conflict pretty much from the start. Tom wanted me to play what he considered modern eighties music like the Eurythmics, who were huge at the time. I understood where he was coming from, not least because my new song, "Five Long Years," could be seen as fitting into the Bryan Adams/eighties pop category easily enough. I think, too, that he was bored with straight blues, perhaps burnt-out on it after working with Clapton on quite a few records. He'd been there, he'd done that, and as I started to get that message, I began to worry more and more. Our age gap of almost forty years didn't help, and neither did my comparatively left-leaning politics, which felt out of step with Tom's Reagan-tinted vision of America in the eighties. Artistic, personal, and political tension—a tough combination to overcome.

We spent money fast, chewing through studio time and resources, and we didn't have much to show for it. It felt, too, like we were light on songs that could break out as hits, so I was desperately trying to write new material, thinking that if I could come up with something with a swampy, Southern feel, it might be a contender. One day I was noodling around and I happened on a riff that I really liked. Could this be the answer? I decided it could be, and I poured all my energy into that riff, subconsciously deciding that it could be the basis for a song that might somehow save this whole troubled project. I phoned Steve and told him that I thought I was on to something, and that I was going to call the song "Voodoo Thing." This was greeted by a sustained silence, long enough for me to start to get nervous.

"Colin . . . I don't think . . . you can't call it that . . . " Steve finally said.

"Why not? It's a great title!" I said.

"Yes, so great that it basically already exists . . . 'Voodoo Chile' . . . 'Voodoo Thing' . . . People will think you're ripping off Jimi Hendrix!"

"I don't think that's a problem, Steve," I said. "They're different tempos, different songs, and aside from that one word, they don't have much in common."

I've been wrong about many things over the years, but this wasn't one of them. I told Steve I was sticking with the title and overruling his objection. In hindsight, I'm so glad I did. I trusted my gut, and my gut was right. Now I just had to convince Tom that the song should make the record.

We played it for him the next day, and he liked it well enough—he thought it had merit, at least, and was worth chasing down. But he had one big criticism: He thought my vocal approach was wrong, and I didn't need to sing it so aggressively. He suggested, instead, that I do a talk/whisper-type thing, à la Tony Joe White. This might have been good advice, but I had no idea what Tony Joe White sounded like, so then we had to listen to a bunch of his songs so I could get my head around the suggestion. The late Tony Joe White was a distinct and excellent singer and songwriter, but he couldn't be further from my natural approach, especially in those early days. I tried to sing/talk like him again and again, take after take, thinking that if I just kept pushing, we might make it work. It happens that way sometimes—you just keep on trying past the point of exhaustion and boredom, and then somehow, magically, something shifts, and something new and exciting just *happens*. But this was not going to be one of those days. We pushed and pushed and just got more exhausted and frustrated. In the end, I had to be as forceful with Tom as I'd been with Steve about the title. I told him that I thought the vocal had to be energetic and loud and in your face, the way it had been when I conceived it. We finally did it my way, and we had something good, a song in which you could feel enough excitement to perhaps save this drowning record.

That small success introduced a new wrinkle into the ever more strained dynamic between me and Tom. Our new "Voodoo Thing" was sounding pretty good, which meant, in a sense, that I'd been right, so the distance between us grew a little wider—he didn't seem to enjoy being wrong (who does!). We kept on trying to work through it, even though it was clear to both of us that we weren't getting anywhere. Challenging creative relationships can sometimes feel like slow-motion car crashes—you're pulled forward by the momentum of the incompatibility, feeling helpless to stop it, and then just get kind of stuck in the gradual dissolution of what was once a promising beginning.

The tensions came to a head when it was time to record what should have been our easiest track, "Why'd You Lie." We all knew it was a great song; we'd been playing it live for two years, audiences loved it, and we'd found radio success with the previous version we'd recorded with Bob Rock in Vancouver. What could go wrong? It turns out it can be hard to top success, and we struggled to best the single we'd already cut. Take after take was deemed inadequate; no matter how hard we tried, they just didn't seem to have the magic. After great effort, we got a decent version of a bed track that we all liked—drums and bass down—and you could sense the whole room relax a bit. We were finally getting somewhere, and we were in familiar territory now, feeling our way through a song we knew, trying to make it a little bit better than it had been before.

We were all sitting in the control room listening to the playback when a look of absolute horror crossed the tape operator's face. No sound was coming on playback.

"Simon, what's wrong?" Tom asked, trying to stay cool.

There was a long silence, and it was as though the air itself curdled.

"You're not going to believe this . . . " Simon said.

"Believe what?" said Tom, a bit less cool this time.

"I have somehow erased everything on this take. I am so sorry. I'm not sure how it happened."

That was it. We were cursed. I called Steve in Vancouver and told him we needed to make a change. I was nervous about making the call, but I knew it had to be done—I had enough of a self-preservation instinct even then, and I knew this wasn't working. It was an expensive way to learn the price of artistic incompatibility, but it was a lesson I'd keep with me for the rest of my days. Going forward, I knew it was important that whoever I was working with had to be on the same page as me from the very start—conceptually, stylistically, and almost most importantly, personally. You can have varying taste, even disagreements, but when you are working together on something, you can't be at cross purposes, cancelling each other out.

Although my experience with Tom Dowd was fraught and difficult, he did have some sage wisdom. Towards the end of our time working together he told me about a soulful singer-songwriter from Dallas named Jerry Lynn Williams who he really wanted me to listen to. He painted Jerry as a backwoods eccentric with an uncanny knack for writing hit songs, a kind of "hillbilly" with a voice somewhere between Willie Nelson and Stevie Wonder. Tom gave me three cassettes full of unrecorded demos that I unceremoniously disregarded—once again the folly of hard youth worked against me. Hidden amongst the many songs on the demos were the titles "Pretending," "Running on Faith," "No Alibis," "Breaking Point," and "Anything for Your Love." You might recognize those songs from Eric Clapton's Grammy-winning return to form album, *Journeyman*, which would come out the next year. Perhaps I should have listened to those tapes at the time!

After considering a few options, we ended up going with a New York City–born, LA-based producer named Danny Kortchmar. Danny had played guitar for James Taylor for many years and at that time was best known for his recent work producing for Don Henley, as well as his cameo in the cult classic *This Is Spinal Tap*. He played Ronnie Pudding, the band's original bassist. Danny didn't have a robust body of work spanning decades the way Tom did, but he seemed like a good choice to me, and we agreed on some important things, such as the sounds of the drums. This was still the era where drum sounds were laden with reverbs and gates, but that tide was just starting to turn and there was a bit of demand for drum sounds that sounded more like . . . well, more like drums. I wanted our instruments to sound like themselves, and I thought Danny might be the guy to help us get there. It would mean, however, relocating again—Danny did most of his work at a studio in Brentwood, California, called the Complex. I headed home to Vancouver to kill some time, impatiently waiting for the flights to LA so we could finish the album once and for all.

On arrival, we all checked into the famed Hollywood Roosevelt Hotel, which was very popular with musicians and artists at the time. The base of its pool, in fact, had just been covered in a gigantic, squiggly mural by the famous painter David Hockney, and it was a quintessentially LA scene. Being at that hotel felt like living inside a movie, in the best way. It wasn't pretentious, but it oozed a relaxed and effortless kind of Californian cool that I was really starting to get a taste for. We'd be living at the hotel for at least the next few weeks, so the band and I settled in and hit the deck chairs. Margaritas for everyone! We needed them by that point.

Our first day at the Complex was incredibly exciting, and it felt as if there were famous musicians around every corner. I shared an awkward hello with Emmylou Harris in the hallway and somehow struck up a friendship with Richie Hayward, who was there recording with someone. He and I would stay in touch and later I'd tour the southeastern United States, all the way to Richmond, Virginia, opening shows for his band Little Feat. With Danny at the controls, we set up in one of the bigger bed tracking rooms and started repairing what we could from the Miami sessions, re-recording things where we needed to and just getting our heads around what we had to work with. Soon enough we began to work again on "Voodoo Thing," which I now hoped would be a contender for a rock radio single. I was determined to stick to my vision and ignore Tom Dowd's advice to try and whisper the song. Danny had no problem with my approach. I set up with a Mesa/Boogie amp to record the bed tracks, and the band and I tore through a few versions of the song until our new producer felt we had what we needed. Compared with everything in Miami, which had been such a struggle, this felt effortless, though of course it was still hard work.

One day I opened the door to the control room to find none other than Bob Seger himself sitting there with Danny, listening to playback on our work. I've been lucky enough to experience a lot of "pinch me" moments over the years, but that one stands out for sure. While we were working at the Complex, I also met another friend of Danny's, a pillar of the LA music scene, the guitar player Waddy Wachtel. Like Danny, Waddy had played with James Taylor. He'd also played with Linda Ronstadt, Randy Newman, Stevie Nicks, Carole King, and so many others, including my one-night-only bandmate Maria Muldaur. A few years later I'd go on the road with him, opening for Keith Richards when Waddy played in Keith's backing band, the X-Pensive Winos, but that's a story for another day.

Everything felt right in LA, and I was psyched to be surrounded by so many extraordinary musicians. I loved working there, but I also loved just *being* there. Those weeks were the beginning of a lifelong fondness for that city, one that continues to this day. Before that trip, I had always imagined LA as a crime-ridden, smog-cloaked sprawl. But I didn't know about the beautiful smell of jasmine lacing the air, or the constant good weather, or the great shopping on Melrose, or the revolving door of world-class musicians whom you'd just happen to run into around every corner. The city had, and has, a magic. Which isn't to say it is without its difficulties, many of which were painfully on display years later when I happened to be there when the Rodney King verdict came down in 1991 and all hell broke loose.

Once we got in a groove with Danny, things came together quickly, and I started feeling a lot better about the work we were doing. Between "Voodoo Thing," "Five Long Years," and "Why'd You Lie," I thought we had at least three strong singles, which helped me breathe a bit easier. As we reached the end of the recording period, we were finishing off "Five Long Years" when I had an idea. We'd decided to totally ditch Tom's version and rework the Bob Rock–produced version. I was happy with where we'd gotten with it, but I thought it still needed one more element, so I invited my old friend and former bandleader Billy Cowsill to sing background vocals on it. I flew Billy down from Vancouver, and I was so happy to have him there. I think I was proud, too, to have this mentor of mine see how far I'd come. The coolest moment came when Billy and Waddy Wachtel spotted each other at the Complex.

"Billy? Is that you?" an incredulous Waddy asked across the room.

To my great surprise, I watched the two men greet each other with a warm embrace. It turns out Waddy had known the Cowsill family back in Newport, Rhode Island, where Billy was from and where Waddy had lived for a time. It made me so happy to think that my record was inadvertently bringing these old friends together.

In those days, the very best way to listen to mixes of new tracks was to have the studio make a cassette of whatever you were working on and then get into your car and blast the stereo. Not only was it fun, it made sense—this is how people buying your music would hear it, so that's how I wanted to experience it, rather than just listening to the pristine sound on monitors in the studio. So, when we'd finish a song, Steve and I would hop in our rental car and drive around Brentwood and Beverly Hills, blasting "Five Long Years" or "Voodoo Thing," which Steve finally seemed to accept had to be called that. I remember those drives so fondly now. Right on the cusp of so much, yet still alone with what I'd made, imagining how it would go into the world, how it would be heard. We'd cruise through the perfect LA streets, golden-hour light hitting all the palm trees, the sound of my guitar flowing out of the speakers and mixing with the soft air. It was perfect, really.

We finished almost everything in LA with Danny, and he was a pleasure to work with. We saved one song for a producer named Neil Dorfsman to mix. Neil had worked with Dire Straits, and because of the style of the song in question, we thought he'd be perfect for the final mix. It was a track called "Dream of Satin," and while I now dislike the song—in fact, I'm a little embarrassed by it—it was very much of its time, and we knew Neil was the guy to make it work. Did it matter that he was in New York, and so we'd need to take our money-burning roadshow to a third major American city to finish this thing off? It did not. We figured we'd spent way too much on the record already, so why stop now. If I could have a word with young Colin on that subject now, I would offer some friendly advice: Neil Dorfsman's production will not make your song any better, save your money!

So, for our last act, we headed to Manhattan, and settled into the legendary Electric Lady Studio, perhaps the most famous studio in the world: commissioned by Jimi Hendrix, home to Stevie Wonder and Lou Reed and the Rolling Stones and David Bowie and U2 and Lady Gaga and Taylor Swift. And, for a short time in the eighties, Colin James! I stayed right off Washington Square, where all the folkies used to hang out in the sixties, and soaked up the whole scene. Neil was a great guy, and the ghost of Hendrix was everywhere in that little studio. Heady stuff, and a fitting way to end an epic, and epically expensive, adventure.

Having a big record contract was a great thing in many ways, but it also left me in the hole. Record companies give you an advance when they sign you, which means an advance payment against future royalties; I'd have to earn that advance back fully before I'd see a dime more. And between Miami and LA and New York, we spent a *lot* of money making the record, money that would have to be earned back too. All told, it cost just shy of US$300,000 to make, and that was before you started adding in extra costs like music videos, which, thanks to the rise of MTV and MuchMusic, were basically obligatory at that point in time. It was expected that every single that went to radio would be accompanied by a video, and they were very expensive, carrying an average price tag of $100,000 or so a pop back then. Sometimes that number went even higher, depending on a record company's belief in a song's potential. That sounds great, doesn't it? The company likes the song so much they're expanding the already huge video budget! But like recording costs, that's just money being fronted by the company, and it adds to the debt you have to earn back as part of recouping your advance and expenses. If you calculate that I would have made around $1.75 from every $20 CD sold, and you figure that, all told, I had to recoup about $600,000 of record company money, that would mean I'd have to sell over a million records to see any further profit from royalties. Even in the heyday of big hair and big debuts, that was a tall order.

But those worries were still further down the road. Back home in Vancouver, and in fact across Canada, you could start to feel excitement building about my debut. As release day neared, it was easy for all of us to get swept up in it. We made the first video, for "Voodoo Thing," in Vancouver before the single went to radio, with a charismatic LA-based video director/choreographer named Eddie Baytos, who at the time was well-known for his recent work on the very successful "Legs" video by ZZ Top. Eddie flew to Vancouver and spent a day finding extras and some local adult dancers for the shoot, which was to feature the band playing the song before a rapturous audience in a club. We filmed it at the excellent Vancouver blues room the Yale. Sadly, it's now a country bar featuring a ridiculous mechanical bull, but the hotel's neon sign lives on as it was given heritage status by the city. The added "Live Blues Nightly" part of the sign was left intact, which makes it even sadder that the club is gone. Vancouver's music scene could really use a room of that size, so I hope one day it returns to its glory as a live music venue.

Filming that video was made even more special because of a VIP guest: my Grandma Kay, who by then had moved back to Vancouver's West End after Grandpa Joe died, and who joined us on set. She had a blast, but she did note with a touch of amusement that it seemed some of the female dancers were wearing nothing at all! It was a great shoot, full of friends, family, and the whole band, and we all agreed it really captured the manic energy of our live shows in those days.

We made two other videos after that, both in Los Angeles, for "Five Long Years" and "Why'd You Lie." The latter was filmed at the iconic A&M studios at the corner of La Brea and Sunset, the very lot that had been built by Charlie Chaplin himself, where he shot many of his classics, including *The Gold Rush* and *Modern Times*. A&M Records had taken it over in the sixties. Years after I filmed that video there, I would end up in LA recording with the late French superstar Johnny Hallyday and be lucky enough to get an invitation back to A&M to play some Ping-Pong with Chuck Leavell and witness the Rolling Stones making their album *Voodoo Lounge*—but I'm getting ahead of myself. After its long history with A&M, it became the Jim Henson lot, home of the Muppets, before recently being bought by musician John Mayer and the film director McG. I hope they kept the Ping-Pong table!

As release day drew near, the label had me start doing advance press, talking to newspapers and magazines from all around the world. This was its own crash course, because talking well in an interview is a skill, and one I had to learn quickly at the tender age of twenty-three. Soon enough I got the hang of it, and each and every conversation got me more amped. Most of the journalists had been sent the record in advance, and it was exhilarating to speak with people about the music and to gauge their reaction. It was a whole new world for me, and it was tremendously exciting to see something building, to watch the hype and hyperbole rise as these songs made their way into the world, taking on lives of their own, connecting with people. I felt humbled and proud in equal measure. And I felt ready for whatever was going to come next.

The release was set for August 13, 1988, four days before my twenty-fourth birthday, and I had high hopes. When you're young and on the verge of a huge moment, you know life will be different. But what you don't know—you *can't* know—is that it will change things so much more than you could possibly imagine, in ways big and small, and in ways that still reverberate to this day. Soon enough I'd no longer be living hand to mouth. My unruly, gravity-defying quaff of hair, leather jacket, and cowboy boots would make me recognizable wherever I went, and I would no longer have to worry about coming up with cash to get into a club, because they'd all let me in for free. Gone would be the days of borrowing twenty bucks from friends, of bumming smokes from people all the time, of borrowing guitars to record. In fact, soon enough guitar companies would be *giving* me guitars, just hoping I'd play them onstage. Of course, all of that would come with its downsides too. The intense and sudden pressure of that kind of fame is hard on anybody, especially someone as young as I was, and the physical demands of constant touring and press would end up wearing even a young me out.

The record would go on to be a big success—it would become the fastest-selling debut album in Canadian history, have three number one videos on MuchMusic, and I would go on to win my first Juno for Most Promising Male Vocalist. But everything about the evolution of the album would also teach me so many hard lessons about the music industry. It's one thing to be a creative musician honing your craft, but it's entirely another to navigate the music business at the same time. I was young, naive, and ill-equipped to look after my best interests when it came to the recording and publishing contracts—I should have sought separate counsel for that. There are more than just a couple of sharks wading in the shallow end of the music business pool, so arm yourself with knowledge early, because things can happen quickly and you may need to make hard decisions fast.

Challenges aside, that record would take me all over the world, touring England, France, Scandinavia, and Greece, as well as just about every town in Canada and many more in the US. It would put me on stages with Keith Richards and with Little Feat. Joyfully, it would reunite me with Stevie Ray Vaughan at an amazing show at the Wiltern Theater in Los Angeles, where Band of Gypsys drummer Buddy Miles would jump up on stage to play with Stevie for a couple of songs. I'd make my New York City concert debut at the legendary Radio City Music Hall, if you can believe it, opening for Steve Winwood for five straight nights. How's that for nerve-racking! And it would lead me to a decades-long career full of so many ups and downs and triumphs and heartbreaks, full of profound friendships and glorious music, a career in which I still have the fun camaraderie of touring with great bandmates (usually a fair bit younger than me these days), playing shows that keep me growing and learning, writing new songs and making new records, and continuing to explore all there is for me in music.

And, in many important ways, it would lead me to the life I have now, and to my greatest joy, my wonderful family—my extraordinary wife Heather May, our hilarious and kind kids, Deghan and Ryland, and, as I write these words, four scruffy dogs who complicate and enrich our lives every day. All of this started the day my first record went on sale. Or maybe it all started the day Stevie Ray christened me Colin James. Or maybe the day I wrote "Five Long Years" on that bench in Vancouver. Or maybe the day my parents bought me my first guitar. Or maybe when I picked up my brother's leftie acoustic. Or just maybe it was when I heard music echoing through our little house in Regina before I could even really open my eyes. A life lived with music, a life lived with love.

It was August 1988, and everything was about to begin for me. But that? That's a story for another day . . .

ACKNOWLEDGEMENTS

Firstly, I would like to send a heartfelt thank you to Jared Bland who was pivotal in the writing of this book. He brought a thoughtful, calming, and organized presence to what could have been a very daunting process. His insights, humour, and patience were truly valuable, and I enjoyed every Zoom call, get together, and writing session along the way.

I would like to thank my parents, Joyce and Bill Munn, for raising four kids so well on their social worker paycheques, and for their contagious passion for life, music, art, and all other things creative. Thanks to my brother, Robbie, and my sister, Cathy, for sharing their memories, and for taking the time to read the manuscript and help me verify some details and timelines, and to my uncle Doug Buck and Aunt Moe for historical clarity in some areas. Thank you to Lorna Janz and Mel Dickin for sharing family photos.

Thank you to Caroline Ackerman for taking me in when I really needed it. Thank you to Chris Gudgeon for introducing me to the book world, and for his help and encouragement from the very start. Thanks to Kerry Gold for starting me down memory lane at the beginning of the process, and to Dana Gee for interviewing my mom about our Ameripass trip.

At Penguin Random House Canada, thanks to Scott Sellers, Sue Kuruvilla, Matthew Flute, John Sweet, and Kristin Cochrane. Thank you to Michelle Findlay and Jane Samis for their tireless work behind the scenes, and to Michael Levine for his guidance.

Thank you to Leanne Campbell and Danielle Burki for keeping our heads above water. Special thanks to Kate McBride and Ryland Munn for their early read through and thoughtful comments. A huge thank you to Deghan Munn Lachnit for always being so supportive. Last and not least, of course, thanks to my wife, Heather, for her pivotal help and encouragement in getting this to the finish line.

COLIN JAMES OBC is one of Canada's most beloved musicians. With twenty-one studio albums, eight Juno Awards, thirty-one Maple Blues Awards and multi-platinum sales, he continues to gain legions of fans around the world with each new record release and his sold-out tours. He's attained seven gold-certified albums during his career, including four platinum albums and two double platinum albums.

Over the years Colin has worked with some of music's most revered artists, including Bonnie Raitt, Albert Collins, Pops Staples, Robert Cray, Albert King, Keith Richards and Buddy Guy, to name but a few.

In 2013, he was inducted into the Canadian Music Industry Hall of Fame and in 2024 was appointed to the Order of British Columbia for his contribution to shaping Canadian music.

Colin James lives in Vancouver, BC.